SHORT WALK

Herefordshire Pubs

David Hinchliffe

COUNTRYSIDE BOOKS
NEWBURY, BERKSHIRE

First published 1996
© David Hinchliffe 1996

COUNTRYSIDE BOOKS
3 Catherine Road
Newbury, Berkshire

ISBN 1 85306 416 5

Designed by Mon Mohan
Cover illustration by Colin Doggett
Maps and photographs by the author

Produced through MRM Associates Ltd., Reading
Typeset by Paragon Typesetters, Newton-le-Willows, Merseyside
Printed by J. W. Arrowsmith Ltd., Bristol

Contents

Publisher's Note

We hope that you obtain considerable enjoyment from this book; great care has been taken in its preparation. However, changes of landlord and actual closures are sadly not uncommon. Likewise, although at the time of publication all routes followed public rights of way or permitted paths, diversion orders can be made and permissions withdrawn.

We cannot of course be held responsible for such diversion orders and any inaccuracies in the text which result from these or any other changes to the routes nor any damage which might result from walkers trespassing on private property. However, we are anxious that all details covering the walks and the pubs are kept up to date and would therefore welcome information from readers which would be relevant to future editions.

Area map showing the locations of the walks.

Introduction

Few things in life are so simple yet so fulfilling as a stroll in the countryside combined with a quiet drink and a pleasant meal in a village pub. This book picks out 20 short, interesting walks, all in attractive surroundings and with much to see along the way – and all starting and finishing at a welcoming pub.

Herefordshire is a walker's delight, with varied scenery and less concession to modern roads, buildings and ways of life than much of England. There are still green pastures over which herds of glossy-coated chestnut and white Herefordshire cattle proudly wander. Also to be found are flocks of sheep, but a far more cosmopolitan bunch than in days of yore, when the Ryland sheep held sway. Such was the wealth they generated for the Leominster area that the wool here was known as 'Lemster ore'.

Other traditional landscape features are apple orchards and hop yards. The farmhouse cider industry was in major decline in the 19th century, but was effectively rescued by Percy Bulmer in 1887, when he founded his famous firm. Their Hereford factory is fed on locally grown apples and produces internationally known brands such as Strongbow and Woodpecker. Smaller producers add variety to the tastes and flavours to be sampled in the pubs or sometimes direct from a local farm.

The hop industry has not found such a saviour, and is much reduced from its Victorian heyday. There are still hops grown however. The hop kilns (the equivalent of Kentish oast houses) may not be used these days, but their distinctive profiles make a mark on many a skyline.

Woodlands and hedgerows continue to grow vigorously, so this is a county of green aspects, watered by tranquil brooks and gentle rivers. Queen amongst these watercourses is the majestic Wye. Every shore it touches is blessed with beauty. Our walks take us along the banks of this and other rivers, as well as the countryside described above.

Most of our walking is on field paths and tracks. The County Council has worked hard at signing all rights of way and putting in place new stiles and footbridges. In a sparsely-populated county such as Herefordshire it is important that as many people as possible use these paths, to keep them open for all to enjoy. The walks in this book have been carefully chosen to reduce the risk of an obstruction spoiling your day, but in high summer the vigorous undergrowth may try to drag you back in places – a walking stick can be a useful ally.

Some stretches are on minor roads, but these tend to be very quiet. Farms and cottages are at every corner, many of some antiquity. Black and white ('magpie') buildings are a particular delight and every village seems to have a story to tell. History there is, today's quietness disguising the often turbulent past, of which ruined castles are just one reminder.

Off the routes, but nearby, are many other visitor attractions, which can be combined with the walks and pubs to give a really enjoyable day out.

A few years ago the country pub seemed doomed, with declining trade and wholesale closures by the national brewers, but many have bounced back with new vigour. Some which closed have been reopened by imaginative new landlords and most have recognised the need to cater for the whole family, so children's play areas and menus are now far more common.

The range of pubs in this book varies from ancient inns in secluded locations to newly modernised ones with surprising themes. Similarly, whilst good, honest, traditional fare is available, I have been amazed at the range of cuisine some pubs are offering, more often than not home-cooked rather than frozen and microwaved. Singaporean, Mexican, baltis, Cajun, Indian – at times researching this book seemed more like a world tour than being on my own doorstep.

One note of warning involves the leaving of cars in pub car parks while you go for a walk. It is advisable that you do alert the pub of your intentions, especially if you are going for a walk *before* you visit the pub. And of course the pub will expect to entertain you at some time during your visit!

I hope you enjoy the walks and the pubs as much as I did, and if we all do our little bit to keep our paths and our pubs open then our heritage will remain secure.

David Hinchliffe
Spring 1996

7

① Mortimer's Cross
The Mortimer's Cross

Mortimer's Cross lies at the important intersection of the Hereford to Knighton road with routes to Presteigne and Ludlow, just as the river Lugg bids farewell to the hill country to traverse the Herefordshire plain. It bears the name of the Mortimer family, the powerful Marcher lords of medieval times, virtually kings in this remote area. One of their bases was just north of here at Wigmore Castle, with another at Ludlow. The culmination of the family fortunes came one cold February day in 1461, when the 19 year old Edward, son of the late Duke of York, led his army to a famous victory on the fields near here.

The inn is on the crossroads, with a sign to remind passers-by of that fateful day. It has been a welcome place of refreshment for many years and although substantially extended over the centuries the original building dates back to 1461. There is a separate poolroom, and the presence of the Battles Bistro indicates that food is high on the list of priorities.

A range of traditional, home-cooked food is supplemented by

house specialities. A 12 oz or 24 oz steak marinated in garlic and mixed herbs, served with sauté potatoes, lamb steak or plaice Dieppe, for example. If you really want to enter into the spirit of things, Lancastrians are presented with Mortimer's beef in red wine and Yorkists can respond with chicken in white wine and herbs. Children's meals are also available. Tetley, Aylesbury and Ansells Bitters are well supported by regularly changing guest beers. Guinness, Kilkenny and Castlemaine XXXX are on offer, alongside Carlsberg Export and Labatt's lagers. The choice in ciders is between Strongbow and Scrumpy Jack. There is an extensive wine list, with prices ranging from economical to the frankly extravagant! The inn provides bed and breakfast accommodation and, for those who bring their own roof, a field for caravans and tents.

The opening hours are from noon to 3 pm every day and, in the evening from 6 pm to 11 pm on Monday to Saturday and 7 pm to 10.30 pm on Sunday. Food is served throughout those hours, but booking is advised for the bistro.

Telephone: 01568 708471.

How to get there: The inn is at the junction of the A4110 with the B4362, north-west of Leominster.

Parking: There is a large car park adjoining the inn.

Length of the walk: 4½ miles. Map: OS Landranger 149 Hereford, Leominster and surrounding area (inn GR 425636).

This is a walk with history in almost every stride. It starts with a saunter along a former Roman highway, passing the famous battlefield of 1461. Cutting through the village of Kingsland by way of field paths, it joins the serene river Lugg, a charming companion for much of the return journey. In summer there may be an opportunity to visit one of the few watermills that is still in working order. This may be the longest walk in the book, but the going is gentle.

The Walk

From the inn head southwards down the main road, in the direction of Hereford. Very soon turn off right at an unsigned minor road by Blue Mantle Cottage. You are now on Hereford Lane, which follows

9

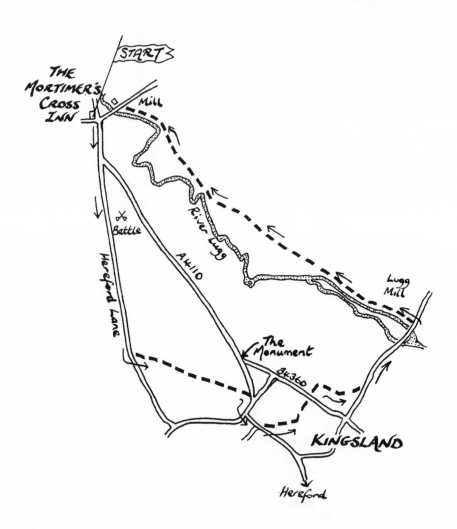

the line of Watling Street West. This was a Roman legionary highway, linking Hereford with Wroxeter in Shropshire.

Just along here and on the left is the site of the Battle of Mortimer's Cross, at the end of the Wars of the Roses. Edward, heir to the mighty Mortimer family, was here in their heartland and his army met the Lancastrian forces under Jasper Tudor at this place on Candlemas Eve 1461. It is said that on the morning of the battle the exceptionally cold weather gave rise to the phenomenon of three suns appearing in the sky. Edward proclaimed this to be a good omen and his forces routed the Lancastrians. Their high-ranking prisoners were taken to Hereford for execution, and Edward duly became King Edward IV at just 19 years of age.

About 100 yards after passing New House Farm you will see a stile on the left. Climb over and make for the far right-hand corner of the field, to another stile. Continue ahead, keeping the hedge on your left. Over the top you may see orchards and then the Luctonians' sports field. Passing to the left of a new house, you will come to the main road.

Go right, along the main road for just over 100 yards and then, off the deep verge opposite the junction with the Brook road, go up some steps and over a stile. Pass through an orchard to another stile. Bear half-right to one more stile, then go through a gate on the left. Cross the field diagonally, to a gap between a house and a bungalow.

At the road you are in Kingsland. A different king this time – Merewald of Mercia, who is said to have had his palace here during the 7th century AD. If you were to walk ¼ mile left to the main road you would see the monument erected in 1799 to commemorate the battle of 1461. A similar distance in the opposite direction are the

The 18th-century monument to a 15th-century battle.

11

earthworks of the castle and the church, but we continue over the road.

Almost opposite, a stile gives access to a garden. Walk along the side to another stile, into a field. Here go right. At the next stile bear half-left, to a stile onto a road. Turn left.

Follow the road, crossing the river Lugg. Turn left onto a track, opposite the Eyton junction. Go through the gate to Kingsland Mill House, bearing left of the house to a stile, then a gate. Initially keep close to the river (actually this is the mill race, diverted at a weir a little upstream).

After passing a farm seen higher up the slope on your right you will come to a stile. Here bear more to the right, to a stile just below the far end of the wood up the slope. Continue across the next field, then drop back towards the river, to another stile.

A gate follows. Now keep ahead as the river bends away to the left. After the next stile there is a small bridge to negotiate, then keep a little to the right and the river will curve back to meet you. Once through the next gate keep close to the river to a stile onto a road.

Almost opposite is Mortimer's Cross Mill. Dating from the 18th century, the mill was in constant use until the 1940s and is still occasionally used. The undershot wheel drives everything – the pulleys, grinding stones and winnowing and grading devices. You can see inside between 1st April and 30th September on Thursdays, Sundays and bank holidays, from 2 pm to 5.30 pm.

Cross the river and continue along the road, and very soon you will be back at the inn, offering a beer garden for warm days and a large open fire in the cosy lounge bar to revive wintertime travellers.

Luston
The Balance Inn

Luston is a charming and well-groomed place, which makes it remarkable that one derivation of the name is 'louse-infested farmstead' and that later it was called 'the dirtiest place you ever did see'. A verse ran, 'Luston short and Luston long, at every house a tump of dung'! Let me reassure you that nowadays it smells as sweet as any village.

What is not denied is that in the whole of the United Kingdom there is only one Balance Inn. It owes its name to its origins as a 17th-century wool weighing station – at that time the area around Leominster was famous for wool ('Lemster ore').

The inn welcomes families and offers a bar with a pool table, dartboard and Sky television. The half-timbered lounge has oak-coloured furnishings, decorated by country kitchen brassware and outside there is a patio area. No one scanning the line-up of drinks will be disappointed by the choice available – Tetley Bitter and Worthington Best are joined by Kilkenny, Bass Special, Caffrey's, M&B Mild and Murphy's. Tennent's Extra and Carling lagers and

13

Scrumpy Jack cider are also here. House wines are supplemented by favourites such as piesporter, liebfraumilch and côtes du Rhone. Food ranges from the truly monstrous, in the form of 32 oz rump steaks, to children-sized meals. The latter include main courses such as fish fingers, followed by an ice-cream and a soft drink. Among the adults' choices there may be home-made curries and vegetarian meals (try the broccoli and cream cheese bake), as well as sandwiches and jacket potatoes. Sunday lunches are popular, bringing the converted barn restaurant with inglenook fireplace into full use.

Opening hours on weekdays are noon to 2.30 pm (except Monday lunchtime, when the inn is closed) and 7 pm to 11 pm. On Saturday the times are noon to 3 pm and 7 pm to 10.30 pm. On Sunday there are full lunches only and no food in the evening. Telephone: 01568 611134.

How to get there: Luston is situated on the B4361 between Leominster and Ludlow. The Balance Inn will be found in the village, which is some 2½ miles from Leominster, south of Richard's Castle.

Parking: There is a car park to the side of the inn.

Length of the walk: 3¾ miles. Map: OS Landranger 149 Hereford, Leominster and surrounding area (inn GR 486632).

This walk is quite easy going (other than a few muddy patches following rain). After calling at Eye church, which has several interesting features and stands alongside a dignified manor house, built out of rather dubious earnings, the return is along field paths and a country road. It would be possible to detour to take in nearby Berrington Hall, but the ideal is to do the walk in the morning, visit the inn for lunch, and spend time at the Hall in the afternoon.

The Walk
Turn left as you come out of the inn car park. On the left you will pass Tudor House, a grand half-timbered building, although of Jacobean rather than Tudor origins. Immediately afterwards, opposite the Methodist chapel, a footpath sign points off to the left. Once you are through the gate there is a grassy track. Cross a

14

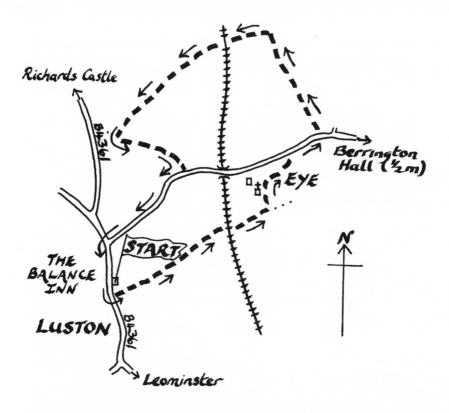

stile and bear slightly left of straight ahead over the field, to a gate. You may catch a glimpse of the white radome on the summit of Titterstone Clee, ahead in the distance.

From the gate aim a little further left to a footbridge. Now keep the field side to your left and carefully cross the railway line. Carry on ahead and go over a track via gates on either side. After another 70 yards turn left over a stile. The next stile facing this one adjoins a ha-ha, a sunken fence that would have kept farm animals from the environs of Eye Manor without spoiling the view.

Enter the churchyard and go round to the other side to enter by the porch. Like most churches, St Peter and St Paul is an amalgam of styles, in this case largely from the late 12th to the 17th century. There is some interesting carving, for example the tie-beam of the central truss in the roof of the nave and the grotesque animals on the pulpit. Among the monuments is one to a Lord Mayor of London.

On leaving the church pass through the lychgate and divert a little to the left. From here there is a good view of the façade of Eye Manor. It was built between 1673 and 1680 for Ferninando Gorges, a Barbados slave trader known as the King of the Black Market. The simple exterior of the house gives no clue as to the lavish interior. The moulded ceilings are a particular delight – that of the entrance hall comprising nine panels, each with swags of drapery, flowers and fruit. Others are no less impressive, with a variety of geometric and naturalistic designs. Alas, they are rarely open to public inspection.

Facing the lychgate of the church is a gate in the fence. Go through and head for the far left-hand corner of the field, where a stile will bring you out onto a minor road. Go right. Opposite a junction with another minor road have a look over into the field on your right. Here you will see the dry bed of the Leominster Canal. Work commenced in 1791, with the aim of linking Kington with the river Severn at Stourport, but all that resulted was a short stretch from Leominster to Tenbury.

Turn left to the farm road (tarmac) opposite the canal bed past two farms. After the second one notice a parallel track in the field on the left. At the point that this bends sharply left, go through a gate to join it, then walk down the field to cross a stream and pass through another gate. Now keep the field side on your left until you carefully cross the railway, the main line between Shrewsbury and Hereford, opened in 1853.

Keep the hedge to your left again, until a bridge enables you to cross the little stream. Continue, with the field side now to your right. The hedge is largely a mixture of hawthorn, hazel and willow. In the autumn you may be accompanied by a foraging party of tits and finches along here.

Go right into a field by a gate at the point the accompanying stream bends sharply in that direction. Walk down the left margin of this field (not quite the right of way, which is a little to the right, but which becomes blocked). At the field corner go through the gate on the left. At the end of the next field pass between two houses and cross a stile.

Now bear to the left of the village hall ahead, to reach a stile onto a minor road. Go right to come into Luston once more, then left to find the Balance Inn.

Berrington Hall.

Places of interest nearby

Berrington Hall (National Trust) is a fine Georgian mansion with a classical portico. The painted ceilings and the full height staircase hall, surmounted by a glass-topped lantern, are especially attractive. The grounds were laid out by 'Capability' Brown and there is a walk through them. Open for part of each week between April and October. Telephone: 01568 615728.

Bredenbury
The Barneby Arms Hotel

Bredenbury is one of those main road settlements that traffic tends to speed through, with scarcely a sideways glance. This is a pity, especially as it is set in the midst of some most attractive rolling countryside. It is very much a 19th-century estate village, the principle features of which are due to wealthy landowner W.H. Barneby. He built his mansion here, resited the church and gave land for the school, amongst other gifts.

It should be no surprise that the Barneby Arms Hotel bears the name of one who left such a mark on the village. However, it was not always thus. Once it was simply called the New Inn and housed both a post office and a grocer's. This is a little difficult to imagine now, as it looks to be the archetypal Victorian country hotel, cleanly styled behind a large car park. Inside, this comfortable hostelry has a bar where darts, crib and dominoes can be played, a lounge and a non-smoking restaurant. To the side is a lawned beer garden, from where parents may keep an eye on their children on the swings and scramble net.

This is a genuine hotel, but non-residents are the norm and are made very welcome. Most visit because of the establishment's reputation for good food. I must warn you that, although out of the towns, people travel some distance to sample the fare here and it can get quite busy. There is a choice of about a dozen starters, such as seafood pancake, deep-fried Brie, or even green-lipped mussels. These can be followed by any of between 24 and 30 main courses, from familiar favourites like battered cod and roast chicken to a range of fresh fish, including salmon, and locally made faggots. Alternatively, chicken Indienne sounds good and vegetarians will find an appetising selection of dishes – wheat and walnut casserole was just one which I don't recollect seeing elsewhere. At weekends a roast carvery with a choice of three meats and in-season vegetables is extremely popular and it would be wise to book in advance for this. Liquid refreshment is certainly not in short supply either. Draught beers encompass Banks's Bitter, Marston's Pedigree, Hook Norton Best and Wadworth 6X. Cider drinkers are not forgotten, with Stowford Press and Bulmer's Strongbow on offer here. Harp and Kronenbourg lagers and a healthy selection of wines are also served.

The weekday opening hours are from 11 am to 2 pm and 6 pm to 11 pm, with food served from 11.30 am to 2 pm and 6.30 pm to 9 pm. On Saturday the lunchtime opening is extended to 3 pm, and food availability to 2.30 pm and 10 pm at night. The Sunday times run from 12 noon to 10.30 pm, with lunch available until 2.30 pm and evening meals from 7 pm to 9 pm. Oh, yes – and early starters can attend for breakfast every day from 7.30 am to 10 am!

Telephone: 01885 482233.

How to get there: Bredenbury is about 3 miles west of Bromyard on the A44 Leominster to Worcester road, and the Barneby Arms is at the west end of the village.

Parking: There is a large car park to the front of the hotel.

Length of the walk: 2 miles. Map: Landranger 149 Hereford, Leominster and surrounding area (hotel GR 607568).

From the hotel there is a stroll along a dead-end (and, hence, very quiet) country road, with fine views over the rolling

19

countryside. Field paths lead you down into one of the creases in the landscape and back to another minor road. A further path returns you close to the hotel. A peaceful short walk in unfrequented countryside.

The Walk

Take the turning between the Barneby Arms and the service station, signed for Wacton. This is a very quiet road, so stride along, taking in the vast panorama over this green landscape. There are particularly good views to Bromyard Downs, to the right.

You will come to the hamlet of Wacton, seemingly much reduced from earlier times. This is commonplace in this area between

Bromyard and Leominster, where evidence points to a formerly significant population, even in the Iron Age. The Court, which once had a defensive moat remains. There was a church here too, at one time, but nothing survives to be seen from the road.

Go right, over a stile, just after a bungalow and shortly before Wacton Grange. Keep the field side to the right and pass through a gate. Descend to a small stream, the field side now to your left. The stream bed may well be dry. Once over, bear right a little to arrive at a more substantial stream by way of a stile.

Cross into a cottage garden – yes, this is the right of way, but please create as little disturbance as possible. Keep slightly right of straight ahead to a pedestrian gate into a field. Cross the field diagonally to a stone stile in the far corner.

Now keep the hedge on your right to come to a road by way of a stile. Go right. You will pass a lodge house to Bredenbury Court, built of rock-faced sandstone by W.H. Barneby. The Court once employed 14 maids, 3 footmen, a housekeeper, butler, valets, nurses and grooms. Now it is a school. Barneby also demolished the old church which stood in the grounds of the Court and built the new one on the main road. He was responsible, too, for the planting of many of the trees from which we now benefit.

The road dog-legs and you then go through a gate on the right, immediately before a small wood. Keep to the edge of the wood, then pass through a gate on the left. Angle over this field to a gate onto the main road. Go right to return to the Barneby Arms.

Places of interest nearby
Humber Marshes Nature Reserve, off the road to Leominster.

4 Bromyard
The Falcon Hotel

Bromyard has been an important religious and trading centre since at least Anglo-Saxon times. It boasts a traditional High Street, unspoilt by the intrusions of the multiples, and is a place where shopping is still an opportunity to stand and gossip. History is ingrained in the buildings, although sometimes disguised by later alterations.

The Falcon Hotel is one of the finest of these venerable black and white structures, set in a prominent position on the main street. It was built in the early 17th century and a large assembly room was added in the 19th century when it became an important coaching inn. Before the advent of the railways coaches stopped here on their way to distant destinations such as Aberystwyth.

On entering the hotel, there is a room with a pool table to the right and the bar beckons ahead, panelled and with a log fire in winter. Here you will find Tetley Bitter and welcome novelties such as Wood Wallop and Deakin's Royal Stag. Stalwart supporters are Kilkenny and Ansells Bitter, Guinness and Murphy's Stout. The lagers are Heineken and Carlsberg, the ciders Strongbow and Woodpecker. In summer you may prefer to take your drinks out to the suntrap patio beer garden. Snacks are advertised on a blackboard above the bar. They may range from grilled rump steak or gammon and pineapple to lasagne or beef and ale pie. There is a separate restaurant with genuine exposed timbering, comfortably upholstered chairs and framed prints of local scenes. A full restaurant menu is available and nowadays people book in advance for the Sunday carvery.

The bar is open every day from 11 am to 11 pm and snacks are served from noon to 2.30 pm and from 7 pm to 9 pm on Monday to Thursday, 9.30 pm on Friday and Saturday. There is no bar food on Sunday evening.

Telephone: 01885 483034.

How to get there: Approaching Bromyard on the A44 Worcester to Leominster road, turn off just west of the bridge over the river Frome to enter the town centre. Follow the road to the left and the Falcon Hotel soon comes into sight on the left.

Parking: There is a car park for patrons to the rear of the hotel, off Pump Street, and you can also leave your car for limited periods on nearby streets. Longer stay car parks are on the northern side of the town and are signed.

Length of the walk: 3½ miles. Map: OS Landranger 149 Hereford, Leominster and surrounding area (hotel GR 655546).

Here is an opportunity to see some of Bromyard's black and white houses, followed by a stroll in the Frome valley, with interesting reminders of the hop industry. The nervous should perhaps not attempt this walk as evening falls – there are stories of ghostly stirrings at an abandoned church passed on the route!

The Walk
From the front door of the hotel turn right along the High Street, coming to the Market Place, with the Hop Pole Hotel standing back. Pass the Bible House. This doesn't take its name from religious connections, but from a stream known as the Bibble, which now runs underground. Turn right down Sherford, passing the old gaol

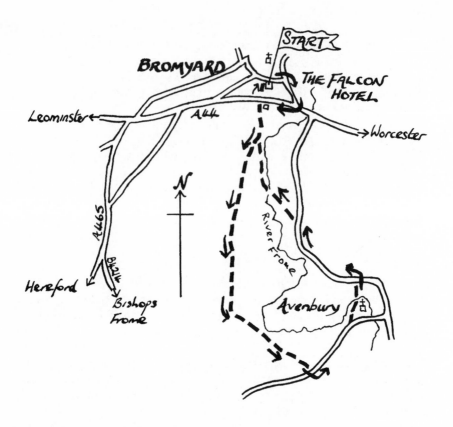

(now a house). At the bottom of the road is the bypass. Before turning uphill to the right, spare a glance over the road to Bridge House, a black and white building dating from the late 16th century.

Further up the hill, at the junction with Pump Street, is a subway to take us to the other side of the bypass. Once over, admire splendid Tower Hill House. Built in 1630, it was still the height of fashion when King Charles I spent the night here whilst on his way to relieve the siege of Hereford in 1645.

Carry on along Tower Hill, crossing the junction with Linton Lane and Highwell Lane. The narrow lane we now take was in use as a route into Bromyard in the Middle Ages. Keep to the left of the building at Little Froome Farm and go through a gate. Stick to the track on the left of a field as it undulates its way to a stile and a gate. Now bear half-left across a field and over a footbridge.

Climb the gentle hill, bearing just left of the red-brick farm ahead. Another stile brings you to the precincts of the farm. To the right are two distinctively cowled hop kilns. Turn left, on the road down the hill. Around here you are likely to see some of the characteristic wirework of the hop yards (fields) where the hops grow. Whilst hop growing these days is but a shadow of its 19th-century glory, the industry still retains a welcome presence in the area.

You will pass a Victorian letterbox in a wall on your left before coming to a footpath sign. Cross the stile on your left and bear half-right towards the river Frome. On your right, shrouded by trees, are the sad remains of Avenbury church – a 12th-century chancel and early 13th-century tower.

Do not be too surprised if you hear the sound of the organ emanating from the ruins. The music, played by the ghost of a local man who was killed by his brother, has been heard by a number of people, including one of the vicars. In medieval times another ghost roamed hereabouts, that of Nicholas Vaughan, who had made the mistake of burning down the Bishop of Hereford's palace.

By the side of the church is a footbridge over the river. Continue to a stile onto the quiet country road, where you go left. After about ⅓ mile there is a stile by a footpath sign on the left. Negotiate the stile and bear diagonally right to the river. A footbridge takes you over – this would make a nice picnic spot, under the trees.

After a stile, keep the river initially to your right, then bear left to a gate to return to the outward track. Go right, back down Tower Hill and under the bypass. This time continue ahead, down Pump Street. Next to the chapel is the Tan House, a reminder of a noxious industry the town doesn't miss.

Places of interest nearby
There is a *Heritage Centre* on Rowberry Street, with exhibits of local interest such as the hop industry. Some 2 miles to the east of the town, off the Worcester road, is *Lower Brockhampton*. This National Trust property comprises a charming group of half-timbered buildings.

⑤ Lyonshall
The Royal George Inn

Lyonshall is a place with a split personality – the church and the ruined castle stand close to the main road between Kington and Leominster while most of the village lies a ½ mile to the south.

When the pub was built in 1600 it was just the George Inn, being renamed when the naval flagship, the *Royal George,* sank at Spithead with the loss of over 900 lives in 1782. Some 150 years ago there were 7 pubs in the village – this one is the sole survivor. Once it had a cider mill, which was supplied by 4 acres of orchards to the rear.

The accommodation includes a cosy lounge and a small restaurant in addition to the public bar, and a very pleasant beer garden with swings for the children. Draught Bass and Worthington Best, Boddingtons, Flowers Best, Murphy's Stout and Stella Artois lager are all to be found on the bar, along with guest real ales. As well as the usual range of sandwiches, salads and other stalwart pub fare the kitchen issues imaginative 'specials'. How about braised pheasant and vegetables or lamb tikka salad and minted yoghurt? Vegetarians may prefer mushroom filled pasta parcels in a garlic and herb sauce. The sweets also tickle the taste-buds, ranging from sorbets, brûlées and mousses to The Governor's Treacle Tart. The four-course Sunday lunch is a noteworthy feature.

The pub is open from noon to 3 pm and 7 pm to 11 pm (to 10.30 pm on Sunday). Food is served from noon to 2.30 pm and 7 pm to 9.30ish pm every day.

Telephone: 01544 340210.

How to get there: The Royal George Inn lies on the A480, which runs between the A438 Hereford to Brecon road and the A44 east of Kington. Lyonshall is about 4½ miles north of the A4112 at Sarnesfield. The inn will be found on the right-angled bend as you pass through the village – it is unmissable!

Parking: There is a large car park to the side of the inn.

Length of the walk: 3¼ miles. Map: OS Landranger 149 Hereford, Leominster and surrounding area (inn GR 337556).

This is a varied walk, largely on a mixture of quiet roads and tracks with paths over fields and through orchards. There is historic interest in an abandoned castle site, a country church and a stretch of Offa's Dyke – a fascinating reminder of the Dark Ages.

The Walk
On leaving the car park turn left, passing in front of the pub, in summer covered with colourful windowboxes. Turn left onto a minor road. This leads out of the village and past Bryncurl Farm on your left. A little further on, a footpath sign on your left, opposite some very functional farm buildings, directs you left and along the field edge to a gateway. Once through you are walking alongside an apple orchard.

The trees are in full bloom in May and the apples are harvested in October, no doubt for the Bulmer's cider factor in Hereford. Leave the orchard by a track over a field to the busy A44. Go left, taking care to remain out of harm's way on the verge. Relief comes after 200 yards, with a kissing-gate on the right. Cross the parkland diagonally left to another kissing-gate. On your right is a picturesque creeper-clad Castle Weir.

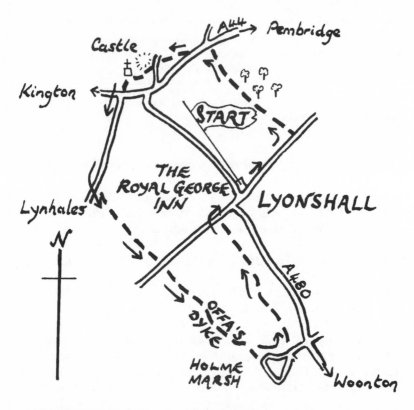

Cross the access road, go over a stile and head up to the woodland edge. Continue to the left. To your right, shrouded by trees are the remains of Lyonshall Castle, thought to have been founded soon after the Conquest. Little can be seen from here when the trees are in full leaf. However, there is a wet moat surrounding a round inner bailey, upon which are the remnants of the keep, probably built about 1220–27, the walls of which are 9 ft thick and 19 ft high. The castle was garrisoned against the Welsh during the 15th century, but then fell into disuse.

A little further on a metal gate on the right leads to the churchyard of St Michael and All Angels. The church has Norman origins, but was heavily restored in the 19th century. Don't be too critical of these Victorian restorers, as in 1869 the building was described as 'in such utter decay as to render it unsafe for public worship'. During renovation an attempt was made to carefully remove the nave roof, but it immediately collapsed.

It is, these days, safe to inspect the features which were saved, such as the grotesque carving of a man's head above the first column of the south arcade, the 13th-century font (on a modern base) and a headless effigy of the same period.

Continue down the path to the main gate, bear left to the road and cross over into the access road to Lynhales Hall. By here was a wharf for the Kington and Eardisley horse-drawn tramway of the 19th century, the access road following the line of the tracks.

Ignore the first footpath sign, but go left, over a stile at the next. Cross the field diagonally to a stile in the right-hand corner. Go left and pass through three gateways, picking up a track which will bring you to a minor road. Opposite is what appears to be a toll cottage. Just to the right of the parking space a path leads by a culvert and over the trackbed of the former Kington to Leominster railway. Go through the facing metal gate, now with the side of the field on your right. At the bottom is a footbridge – once over, go slightly right and make your way uphill, with the field edge now on your left.

Lyonshall church.

29

Spare a glance for the wooded mound at your shoulder. This is no less than a section of Offa's Dyke, built between AD 756 and AD 795. Offa was a mighty ruler of Dark Age Mercia and his forces were engaged in a relentless struggle with the Welsh. Whether the Dyke was a defensive structure or simply marked the previously unidentified border, we do not know. It was certainly a massive undertaking, a ditch and rampart stretching from Prestatyn in North Wales to Chepstow on the Severn Estuary. This is one of the best sections to be seen in the lowlands, where much of it has been destroyed.

Towards the top of the slope go left through a breach in the defences and over a stile. If you glance back you will see a local landmark, the yew trees on Rushock Hill. Eyes forward, bear right of the bungalow to reach the road. Turn left.

Go over a stile on the left at the point where another minor road is joined. Cross the field and at the top of the rise go through the left hand of two gates. Pass farm buildings on your right as you now head down the slope.

Cross a farm track by means of two gates and bear right to the field edge. After climbing a stile in the fence on the right, cross a field diagonally to a half-hidden stile next to some large sheds. Lyonshall church is in view ahead, as you drop down to cross the Curl Brook.

Finally, another footbridge leads to the road, where go right, joining the main road, with the Royal George just ahead.

Places of interest nearby
Kington with its shops and unusual church is just 2 miles away. *Hergest Croft Gardens*, on the edge of the town, boast a fine selection of rhododendrons and azaleas. *Kington Golf Club* is the highest golf course in England and Wales.

⑥ Weobley
The Unicorn Inn

If Herefordshire is the home of the black and white cottage, then Weobley lies at its heart, ancient dwellings leaning crookedly all around. The village is also blessed by an especially fine church with a magnificent spire, which hints at the former importance of this settlement.

The Unicorn Inn dates from the 17th century, with the lounge replacing a 12th-century cider house, so it has a long association with liquid refreshment. Inside it retains much of its original character and is a cosy, friendly place. In winter you will probably find an open fire.

Yes, there are bar snacks and traditional pub fare, but what lifts the cuisine out of the ordinary is the inclusion of genuine specialities from Singapore. Satay (beef or pork), nasi goreng (fried rice) or dried chilli noodles with prawns and vegetables are just some of the exotic tastes on offer. On Sundays you can choose either a roast lunch or any of six different Singaporean dishes. Children are welcome and can have half portions of most meals at half price. As for drinks, John Smith's Bitter is joined by Worthington Bitter and Beamish Stout. Carling lager, Foster's and Stowford Press cider are to be found too. Accommodation is also available and you will be in good company, as King Charles I is reputed to have stayed here.

The inn opens from noon to 2.30 pm (to 2 pm on Sundays) and again from 7 pm to 11 pm. Food is served from noon to 2 pm and 7 pm to 9 pm.

How to get there: Weobley lies on the B4230, which runs between the A480, north-west of Hereford, and the A4112. Turn off east into the village centre. The Unicorn Inn is just past the Market Place, on the left-hand side.

Parking: The inn has a small car park to the side. There is on-street parking around the Market Place.

Length of the walk: 3 miles. Map: OS Landranger 149 Hereford, Leominster and surrounding area (inn GR 403515).

First of all, wander around this lovely village, soaking up the atmosphere generated by many venerable buildings. Visit the church, with its inspiring steeple and curious stories, then stroll through the site of the former castle and across parkland. The walk returns to the inn by way of field paths.

The Walk
Turn right from the inn to return to the Market Place where you turn right. Some of the houses here date back to the 15th century. At the bottom of the street, the Red Lion Hotel is a century older. Carry on down The Pavement towards the church and turn into the churchyard.

The church possesses a number of curiosities. For example, the corbel stones high on the south aisle, one of which seems to depict a man with toothache, and the carving of a rather evil character with a knife or a sword above the pulpit. The tower is at an angle to the main building, the 14th-century font boasts a variety of motifs and

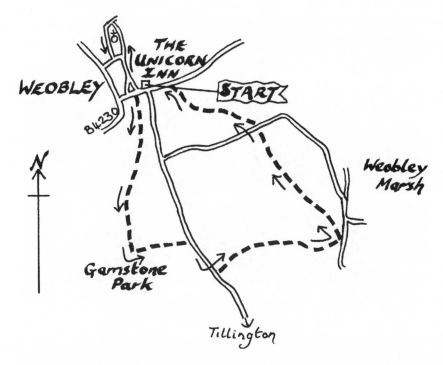

there is a commanding statue of Colonel John Birch, whose life story warrants a book to itself. A successful Roundhead commander during the Civil War, he captured Hereford by stealth. After the war he acquired land and became Member of Parliament for Weobley, frequently falling foul of Cromwell. Later he welcomed back Charles II as king. Birch also financed the rebuilding of the church spire following the collapse of the original. It remains the second highest in the county. Outside, beware the preaching cross – it is reputed that if you walk backwards seven times around each tier of the steps you will see the Devil.

Assuming you have resisted this temptation, on leaving the church porch turn right to Church Road, where you turn left. This will bring you to the charming setting of Bell Square, where the houses are amongst the oldest in the village, some dating back to the 14th century.

Turn left at the bottom of Church Road, then go right to walk up Broad Street, which becomes Market Place. In the triangle of land at the top, now grassed, was once the Market Hall and another

The village of Weobley.

building destroyed by fire in 1943. Here also stood the Mansion House, where in the late 16th century James Tomkins fathered 33 children by 2 wives.

Reflecting soberly upon this information, proceed straight ahead, along a trackway, passing the telephone kiosk. Go through a gate to enter the site of the former castle, built by de Lacys soon after the Conquest. It was besieged by King Stephen in 1138 and was used in the early 13th century by William de Braose in his rebellion against King John. Now only the earthworks remain, surrounded by dry moats.

Carry on through a kissing-gate and bear slightly right through another one. You are now in Garnstone Park. Colonel Birch (remember him?) bought the great house of Garnstone in 1661 and greatly improved it. It was rebuilt by Nash in 1807, but was demolished in 1959.

Somewhere in the Park is a pool containing a snuffbox in which a ghost has been laid, but the author has not sought this out.

Carrying straight on from the kissing-gate, across the parkland, you will arrive at another such gate, but this time turn left in front of it. Continue through a further gate and turn right along the road, in front of a lodge. In the field to the left are some lovely oak and sweet chestnut trees.

Go left at a footpath sign, down the roadway to The Field. Go right immediately before the yard, along the side of a wall, and over a stile. Continue beside the field edge to the left, over a stile and a plank footbridge. Now turn left, along the edge of the field and over a stile. The rights of way in this field veer first to the right of a red brick house and then acutely back to the left to a stile – in other words, this stile is in the hedge to your left as you make towards the house.

Having solved that little problem, the path now continues over fields, across three more stiles. Then, with the field boundary to your left, you come to a short length of lane and so to the road. Cross over to the next stile and head half-left, holding this line over a stile and through a gateway. The next stile brings you to a path at the rear of bungalows.

On arriving at the road turn left, and in a short distance you will return to the Unicorn Inn.

Places of interest nearby

There is a *museum* covering local history off Back Lane. Outside nearby Eardisland (follow the A4112 towards Leominster, then the A44 westwards) is *Burton Court,* an impressive amalgam of styles from Georgian to Edwardian. This exterior hides the Great Hall, which dates from the 14th century. It houses a costume collection and also on display are many curious items collected in the course of world-wide travels by past occupants of the Court.

⑦ Canon Pyon
The Plough Inn

Canon Pyon and neighbouring King's Pyon have a nice, dignified ring to their names. Surprisingly, pyon means 'gnat's island', our predecessors not being the type to mince words. Nowadays the village, as insect-free as anywhere else, stretches out along the A4110, a route north out of Hereford since at least Roman times.

The Plough Inn may have a somewhat shorter history, but nevertheless exudes a gently rustic character. Once inside, it seems larger than on the outside, comprising a bar, a lounge and a restaurant. There are various pub games, including darts, pool and crib, with a skittle alley for the more energetic. Active youngsters are well catered for by an enclosed play area with swings, a climbing net and crazy golf.

The food is all honest, appetising, home-made stuff. Starters include garlic mushrooms and smoked mackerel, and among the main course are steaks and gammon. Vegetarians are not forgotten and will be offered dishes such as cauliflower and potato bake. Sunday lunches are a speciality and children's meals are available.

The draught beers are Bass and Boddingtons, with Caffrey's, Bass Special and Toby also on offer. GL and Strongbow ciders, Tennent's Extra and Carling Black Label are served too. There is a good choice of wines.

On weekdays the Plough Inn opens from noon to 3 pm and again from 7 pm to 11 pm. At weekends it is open from noon to 11 pm. Food is served from noon to 2 pm (except Monday) and 7 pm to 10 pm (except Tuesday).

Telephone: 01432 830577.

How to get there: Canon Pyon lies some 6 miles north-west of Hereford on the A4110, midway between its junctions with the A438 Hereford to Brecon road and the A44 west of Leominster.

Parking: There is a large car park to the side of the inn.

Length of the walk: 3½ miles. Map: OS Landranger 149 Hereford, Leominster and surrounding area (inn GR 463486).

This walk takes us out of the village, to the 'leaning' church. We then gently climb the flanks of Pyon Hill, where legends of ancient heroes and giants abound – and there is the bonus of good views. From here the route descends and returns at a lower level via field paths and a quiet country road.

The Walk
Walk northwards along the A4110. Almost opposite the Wellington junction an unsigned minor road goes off to the left. Follow this for about ¼ mile, then go over a stile on the right at a footpath sign. Keep the hedge to your left, crossing a small stream and climbing the opposite side of this very gentle valley. When you come to the road go left.

Pass the immodestly-named, late-Georgian Great House – it has nice wrought-iron gates. At a sharp right-hand bend go through the churchyard gate ahead. The church stands well outside the village, but is more remarkable for what you find inside. The arcades of columns on either side of the nave lean most alarmingly. It is perfectly safe, having been in this condition since at least the 15th century, and there are reassuring buttresses to take the weight. Also to be seen are some charming carvings of animals, such as a fox,

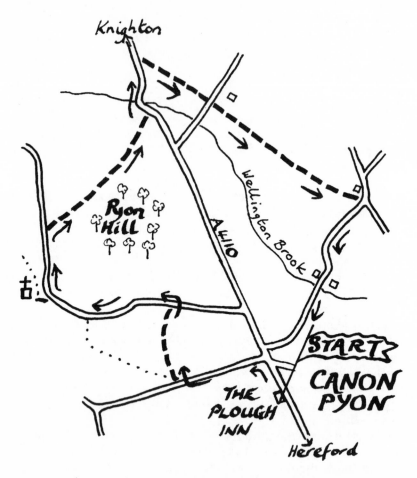

goose, a pelican and so on. These are said to have been taken from
the abandoned abbey at Wormsley, to the south-west, upon the
dissolution of the monasteries.

On emerging from the porch, bear left to return to the road,
where you go left up the gentle slope. Towards the top of the rise
there is a bridleway sign, pointing to the right. Go through the
adjacent gate and continue to ascend gradually, keeping the hedge
to your left. You are here climbing the flank of Pyon Hill and if you
look back you will see its twin, Butthouse Hill. Many stories seek to
explain the existence or the use of these two small peaks, of which
just three are recounted below.

One tale is that Robin Hood and Little John were each carrying a spadeful of earth to bury the monks at nearby Wormsley. Someone told them that they were heading the wrong way, so they abandoned their quest and dropped the earth – some spades! Perhaps this story originated with the dissolution. Another legend is that two giants were jumping over Wormsley Hill and each kicked out a lump of earth – those two lumps being Pyon and Butthouse Hills. One local name for the hills is Robin Hood's Butts, as it is said that the famous outlaw used to fire his arrows across from one hill to the other.

The reality is that both hills are formed of cornstone, which is more resistant to erosion than the surrounding sandstone, but this isn't quite so romantic!

Towards the top of the rise pass through a gate emblazoned with a bridleway waymark. This is a lovely spot, the gradual gain in height being rewarded by views forward to Westhope Hill and back to Garnstone Hill. Alas, now we descend, just left of ahead, with Crookshill Wood to the left. Another waymark guides you to a stile by a gate and then, with the hedge on the left, down to the road, which is gained by means of a pedestrian gate.

Turn left, along the busy A4110, a far cry from its Roman origins. Fortunately, after about 100 yards you can go right at a bridleway sign. Keep the hedge to your left again, to come to a minor road. Cross, then proceed ahead over a field, with Fullbridge Farm to your left. When faced by two gates, go through the one on the left and continue ahead, now with the hedge to your right.

Pass through two more gates, after the second of which the hedge is on your left – ignore a stile and footbridge on that side. The next gate leads into an orchard. Keep to the left to arrive at a minor road. Go right to return to Canon Pyon. At the junction turn left, back to the Plough Inn.

Places of interest nearby
Queenswood Country Park on Dinmore Hill (on the A49 just north-east of Canon Pyon) is a large area of woodland with a beautiful arboretum and a superb viewpoint. Just south of Queenswood is *Dinmore Manor* with many fascinating features – lovely gardens with a curious grotto, medieval sundials, the 12th-century church of the Knights Hospitallers and more.

⑧ Eardisley
The Tram Inn

With so many black and white picture postcard villages to choose from in Herefordshire, Eardisley's charms can all too easily be overlooked. This is one of those cases where one just has to leave the car behind and explore on foot.

The Tram Inn reminds us that in the early 19th century a horse-drawn tram service linked Eardisley with Brecon. Coal was transported from South Wales, with corn and lime travelling in the opposite direction. The arrival of the railways spelled the end for the trams, but the inn survives, now catering for those arriving by more modern transport.

Once inside, you will find a comfortable lounge and a public bar, with a beer garden to the rear. Salads, sandwiches and dishes such as home-cooked chilli con carne are supplemented by hearty meals like the Tram Platter – a jumbo sausage and chips with a sandwich and a salad – just the job when you have worked up a walker's appetite. Another option is the Steak Feast, an 8 or 12 oz sirloin, served with chips, onion rings, mushrooms and salad. The

Tramburger is enormous and is offered with a choice of rice, chips or jacket potato and a salad garnish, as are other specialities, for example venison casserole or mussels and scallops provençale. Children are not forgotten and will enjoy chicken bites, sausage and chips, and similar favourites. Liquid refreshment includes Theakston XB and Best, Younger's Best, Guinness, Coors or McEwan's lagers and Bulmer's Original and Strongbow ciders.

The opening hours are from noon to 3 pm and 6 pm to 11 pm, except on Sunday when the evening times are 7 pm to 10.30 pm. Food is served from noon to 2.15 pm and 6 pm (7 pm on Sunday) to 9 pm.

Telephone: 01544 327251.

How to get there: Eardisley is on the A4111, which runs between the A438, some 13 miles west of Hereford, and the A44 at Kington. The Tram Inn will be found almost opposite the Almeley junction, north of Eardisley church.

Parking: There is quite a large car park to the front of the inn.

Length of the walk: 2½ miles. Map: OS Landranger 148 Presteigne and Hay-on-Wye area (inn GR 310496).

Route-finding is straightforward on this walk, which starts off on a quiet country road to visit the parish's oldest inhabitant. From here field paths and a farm track return you to Eardisley and its famous church. The pride of the village is the ornate Norman font, an artefact of beauty and historical significance. There are Dickensian links as well before we return.

The Walk
From the pub go left, down the road signed to Woodseaves. Notice the black and white cottages on the left, one of which displays the ancient cruck form of construction, using the limb of some sturdy oak tree. Further along this road divert left along Canonford Avenue – in summer you may see some exemplary gardens here.

Continue across the grassed area at the head of the cul-de-sac and bear left, over the bridge. Ignore the road to Welson on your right, but take the next minor road on that side, by the old chapel. Here you will find the Great Oak of Eardisley, reputed to be a remnant of

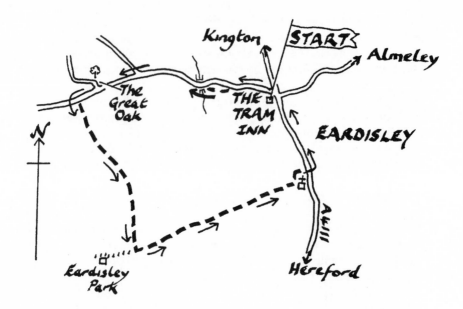

Hurstway Forest which was recorded in the Domesday Book. A fire in the 1950s caused it to be hollowed out, but still it survives.

Return to the road by the chapel and turn right. Now turn left down the private road to Park View. Pass through a gate to the left of the house and keep the field boundary to your left. It can get muddy along here. Cross a footbridge, followed by a gate and then a stile. Now bear half-right across the field to a stile midway along the facing hedge. This leads onto the tarmac drive to Eardisley Park.

We turn left here, but spare a glance for the great house to the right. Built in the early 18th century, it retains the original dovecote and cider house. (You can divert along the bridleway to your right if you would like a closer look.)

The track makes its way into Eardisley. In the woodland on the left are the remains of the castle. This was one of the earliest defended houses in the country. In 1263 the reviled Bishop of Hereford, the grasping Peter de Acquablanca, was imprisoned here by Roger de Clifford, but most of the structure was demolished during the Civil War. Some say that it was a Royalist mob from Hereford who did the damage, others that it was Cromwell's troops, but whoever it was, the result was the same.

You are now faced by the parish church of St Mary Magdalene. Go in, and on your left is the remarkable sculpted font. Along with the font at Canon Frome and doorway at Kilpeck, it is an example of the early 12th-century Herefordshire School of sculpture. Clearly depicted is the lion, symbolising evil. A figure is being pulled out of a thicket by Christ, with the dove on his shoulder. Also represented is a duel, the participants being believed to be Ralph Baskerville and his new father-in-law, Lord Drogo of Clifford. The latter was killed in the combat and Ralph repented so much of his actions that he ended his days as a monk in Gloucester.

The Baskervilles were lords of the manor for 500 years. The family lived at Eardisley Castle from the 13th to the 17th century when their fortunes declined, with the last Baskerville living in genteel poverty in the castle gatehouse. A memorial to one of the Barnsley family of Eardisley House, who succeeded them, is on the vestry wall, opening 'Bubble's broken, but Death's the key to life'. It refers to another rags to riches and back to rags story involving the family over some 34 years and is thought to have formed the basis for Charles Dickens' novel *Bleak House*.

Return through the churchyard gate, then turn right and walk round to the main road. Turn left. At the entrance to Castle Close is a cider press. Continue along the main road to return to Tram Square.

Places of interest nearby
Not too far away, to the south-west, is *Hay-on-Wye*, a pleasant border town on the banks of that lovely river. Its fame rests in being the secondhand book capital of the kingdom. Even for non-bibliophiles a walk around the town to find cinemas and chapels amongst the many buildings pressed into service for this purpose is a must.

9 Cradley
The Red Lion

The village of Cradley lies on the eastern fringes of the county, in the shadow of the Malvern Hills. It has ancient origins and is, interestingly, in two parts. These face each other across the Cradley Brook, and the Red Lion is in neither of them!

The inn is just to the north of the village, at Stifford's Bridge, where the main Hereford to Worcester road crosses the gentle valley of the Cradley Brook. Small rooms have been partly opened out to improve access between them whilst retaining quiet and secluded corners. One may choose between bar, lounge, restaurant, family room and, on warmer days, beer garden and patio. There is also an outside area where children can let off steam. Indoors, crib is played and regular quiz evenings are held.

The level of choice extends to the menu. In addition to standard pub fare there are particular specialities, for example game casserole, pan-fried mussels, vegetarian bake or braised pork and mushrooms in a white wine and sherry sauce. Portions are certainly on the ample side, but try and find room for one of the tasty

44

desserts. Children's favourites such as chicken nuggets and fish fingers, all with chips and peas, are sure to please younger members of the family. As for drinks, Draught Banks's Bitter, Marston's Pedigree, Hobsons Best and, a surprise find, Shropshire Lad are all waiting for sampling. Cider drinkers are not neglected, as Woodpecker, Strongbow and Scrumpy Jack are to be found, alongside Kronenbourg and Harp lagers. There is also a wide choice of house and table wines.

The Red Lion opens each day from noon to 3 pm, with meals served until 2.30 pm. On weekdays and Saturdays the evening opening runs from 6.30 pm to 11 pm and food is available from 7 pm to 9.30 pm. Sunday evening opening is from 7 pm to 10.30 pm, with food served only in summer, between 7 pm and 9.30 pm.

Telephone: 01886 880318.

How to get there: The Red Lion is at Stifford's Bridge on the main A4103 road between Hereford and Worcester. If you are approaching from the west, you will find the pub in a dip about ½ mile beyond the B4220 sign for Cradley.

Parking: There is a large car park to the front of the inn.

Length of the walk: 2 miles. Map: OS Landranger 150 Worcester, The Malverns and surrounding area (inn GR 734481).

Initially the walk keeps the company of the little Cradley Brook – indeed, it never ventures too far from it. On arriving in the village there is a small detour to have a look at some of the quaint features of the church and the ancient school house. The route then crosses the brook again to return to the opposite slopes of this gentle valley, with views over to the Malvern Hills.

The Walk

Leave the pub car park and turn right to cross the Cradley Brook. Immediately afterwards turn right through a kissing-gate. The path now leads through fields alongside the tranquil brook, no doubt with gently grazing sheep around. Keep towards the left of the fields. On passing a house go right, down a tarmac track. The path, which used to run through Wold Mill at the end of this track has been diverted to cause less disturbance. Cross a stile on the left.

45

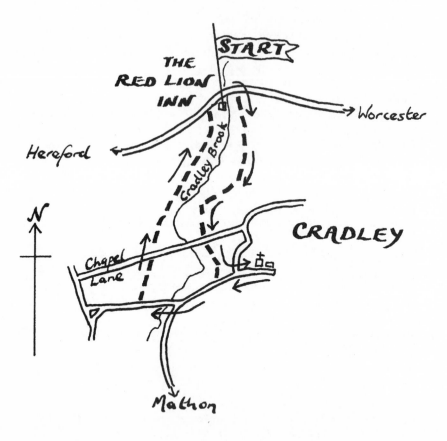

Once over the brow of a small hill you should be able to see a stile ahead, which will bring you onto a lane. Turn right, and very soon on the left is a discreet fence stile. This gives access to a good path, which joins the road by the village school.

Go left, uphill. Once round the bend turn right by the war memorial to approach the church through the timber-framed lychgate. Although the church was extensively rebuilt in the 19th century there is a short length of Saxon frieze set into the north wall of the tower. There is also a 12 ft chest hewn from the trunk of a single tree, and a Georgian font of 1722. A board sets out the penalties for bellringers who do not conform to the rules – for example, those who curse and swear in the bell tower are subject to a fine of sixpence.

Back in the churchyard, the sundial bears the inscription 'Tyme Tryeth Troth'. Does this reflect on the age of the church or the venerable yew tree, which has witnessed events here for 1,200 years?

Mere youngsters leave the churchyard and turn left to have a look at the half-timbered old school house on the left. It is a building for the connoisseur of this mode of construction, but all can admire its grace. A boy's school in 1674, it is now the village hall.

Return down the track and along the road past the school. At the junction go right, to cross the Cradley Brook by way of Kings Bridge. Start climbing the hill ahead but then turn right along a lane. Your head will probably turn towards the flowing lines of the Malvern Hills, away to the right. Those lofty heights are made of far older and sterner stuff than the Old Red sandstone which lies close to the surface of most of Herefordshire.

Cross Chapel Lane and keep along the field side. Bear just left of some houses, over a couple of stiles, then pass through a gate. Presumably, the route once ran in the sunken track on the right of this field, but this has become overgrown by scrubby undergrowth, like so many of these historic ways.

At the bottom of the field the stile is in a corner. Carry on to the road, which may be something of a modern-day shock after the peace of the walk. Turn right and, fortunately, the Red Lion is just a short distance away.

Places of interest nearby
Visit *Great Malvern*, 4 miles to the east, with its beautiful Priory. This houses the best medieval stained glass outside York Minster, fascinating carved misericords and genuine medieval tiles. It is in a lovely setting beneath the hills. Nearby is Priory Park, another delightful spot for relaxing.

⑩ Colwall
The Oddfellows

Colwall luxuriates under a leafy canopy as it shelters at the base of the Malvern Hills. It climbs gradually from the expanse of Colwall Green to Colwall Stone – whether the stone resting at the centre of the village was thrown by a giant on the hills we cannot be sure, however. Further along is the plant where the internationally famous Malvern Water is bottled. The road then rises to Upper Colwall, high on the flanks of those omnipresent hills.

Oddfellows started life as a single storey, thatched hostelry known as the Horse and Groom. At the turn of the century it was expanded and became the Horse and Jockey. It was originally built by Mr R. Cave-Browne-Cave, the driving force behind the now long-defunct Colwall Park Racecourse. The new name, which came with a major refurbishment, completed in 1994, acknowledges the hall to the rear, used by the Order of Oddfellows, the first to be established outside Manchester. The interior is a revelation to anyone who knew the old premises, but retains a simple, traditional feel. The lounge and dining area display rustic brick and timber wainscots, mostly underlain by a polished wood floor. The bar has quarry tiles, a pool table and bar stools made out of milk churns, and the solid fuel stoves relish the constant loving care – and ready supply of firewood – they receive in winter. Outside is a patio and a kiddies' play area. For a longer stay, you can hire a pitch for tent or caravan in the field at the rear or rent the holiday flat.

Theakston ales take pride of place, with the redoubtable Old Peculier flanked by XB and Best and a guest beer. Guinness and Gillespie's provide a choice of stouts, with Beck's and McEwan's lager and Woodpecker and Scrumpy ciders also available. A nice touch is that the wine list is altered to match the menu, which itself changes regularly. Examples of dishes are king prawns in garlic or café de Paris butter to start with, followed by lemon and tarragon chicken breast or pork escalope with gypsy sauce. Vegetarians are well provided for – perhaps ratatouille bake or nut cutlet provençale might appeal. A blackboard lists the specials, desserts and ice-creams, and liqueur coffees make a fitting conclusion to a meal. The children's bill of fare is the best I have seen in the county. Yes, there are chicken nuggets with a choice of dips, but also a number of really imaginative dishes. These include oriental vegetable rice – stir-fried rice, onions, peppers, carrots, bamboo shoots, baby corn, mushrooms, and mangetout – or ocean bake, which comprises tuna, mushrooms, onions, sweetcorn and pasta shells in a sauce topped with breadcrumbs.

The hours vary according to season. In summer Oddfellows is open from noon to 11 pm (10.30 pm on Sunday), but in winter the times are noon to 3 pm and 7 pm to 11 pm (again, 10.30 pm on Sunday). Food is served from noon to 3 pm, extended to 4 pm on summer Fridays and on Saturdays. Evening serving is 7 pm to 9 pm (10 pm on Saturday).

Telephone: 01684 540084.

How to get there: Oddfellows, situated just north of Colwall Green, is alongside the B4218, which runs between the A449 north-east of Ledbury and the B4232 at Upper Wyche.

Parking: There is a large car park at the side of the pub.

Length of the walk: 3 miles. Map: OS Landranger 150 Worcester, The Malverns and surrounding area (inn GR 751421).

On quiet paths in the shadow of the Malvern Hills, this is a languid stroll into the past. Amongst the buildings passed on the way are Colwall's remote church with its rare alehouse (alas, 'dry' nowadays) and a former Bishop's hunting lodge. In summer you may be distracted by the whack of willow on leather at a quality cricket ground, whilst in the distance you watch those toiling along the summit ridge of those ancient hills.

The Walk
To the left of the pub as you face it is a footpath sign. Go over the adjoining stile and turn left, along the field edge. Pass to the side of the village hall and at the road turn right. In a few yards turn left at a footpath sign, along a green lane. This passes the cricket pitch, where each year in mid-August the Women's Cricket Association

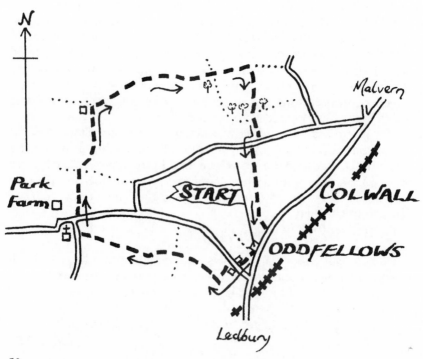

celebrates Cricket Week. The stepped profile of Herefordshire Beacon (British Camp) is prominent beyond the ground.

Pass through a gate. Shortly before the gate out of the large field you have now entered, turn sharply right – the path is usually well defined. Pass through a waymarked gate and then keep the hedge to your right. Most of the familiar hedgerow shrubs are present and in autumn the sloes, crab apples, hazelnuts, haws and acorns make this a veritable natural larder for wild animals and birds.

After a gateway at a bend the hedge will now be to your left. Colwall rectory should be clearly visible ahead. A stile and a gate lead to the road. Turn right and there you will see the half-timbered alehouse, which dates from the early 16th century. Parishioners used to retire here for a reviving drink in mid-service – no doubt longer and less convivial than nowadays. Not surprisingly, the Puritans closed down such establishments in the mid-17th century. Later the building was used as almshouses before falling into disrepair in the 1930s. Fortunately, it was rescued and reopened as a church hall in 1990.

The church itself retains but a few traces of its Norman origins, much of it being 14th century, not least the fine nave roof. Have a look at the brass tablet, dated 1590, on the south wall.

Returning to the road by the alehouse, turn left. Continue ahead at the junction, passing through the gate as directed by the footpath sign. Over to the left is Park Farm. In medieval times this was a residence, probably a hunting lodge, of the Bishop of Hereford, which explains why the church is here rather than in the village. The bishop was involved in a bitter dispute with a neighbouring landowner regarding ownership of deer herds. This led to a dyke being dug along the very summit of the Malvern Hills to prevent deer straying onto the bishop's lands.

The track leads you by pleasant fishponds towards a sewage treatment works. Bear just to the right, over a gate and over a stile. Now go half-right to a plank bridge and stile in the hedge. Once over, head straight across the field, aiming just right of a house. Don't go through the adjoining gate, but instead bear right, along the side of the woodland.

Keep the field side to your left over a series of four stiles. The next one is hidden in a dip. Once over, take care not to go astray – the wood is now immediately to your right. After the next stile look out for one in the hedge on your right. Now keep the margin of

The Alehouse, Colwall.

light woodland to your left and you will come to a stile into an orchard.

Follow the track ahead, through a gateway and so to the road. Turn right, then almost immediately left, down a track. Pass through two gates, then go over a stile ahead at the point the track bends sharply left. For once don't keep too close to the hedge as you cross this field. Pass under both sets of power lines and into a dip in the far corner of the field. Here there is a passage to the left, over the small stream. This brings you to the road, with Oddfellows just to the right.

Places of interest nearby
The *Malvern Hills* are an obvious attraction, with many easy points of access from plentiful car parks. The views across Herefordshire and Worcestershire are superb. *Eastnor Castle*, a 19th-century, pseudo-medieval fortification, is set in lovely grounds about 3 miles to the south. The lavish interiors have been used as sets in a BBC TV dramatisation of *Little Lord Fauntleroy*.

Tillington
The Bell Inn

11

Tillington is a hamlet in the parish of Burghill, lying at the heart of cider orchard and soft fruit country and the Bell Inn stands in a key position for those visiting this area to fill the freezer, make jam, or just to enjoy the blossom.

The inn has a long history, and the original Land Registry documents are on display in the comfortable lounge. You will find a separate bar, a dining room and a pleasant beer garden, where the children really enjoy the play area. There is usually a guest cask ale alongside the regulars, which are Bass, Whitbread WPCA and Wye Valley Bitter. Mind you, there are plenty of alternatives – Boddingtons Bitter, Heineken and Stella draught lagers, Beck's and Kaltenberg Pils. Being in the heart of cider country, you will not be disappointed by the choice of Bulmer's Traditional, GL and Strongbow. Bar wines go beyond the usual, with Australian chardonnay and Rowlands Brooks' reds and whites amongst the tipples available. You might anticipate standard pub fare such as gammon, steaks and roast chicken, but there are also more cosmopolitan options. Baltis and Moroccan chicken, for example, and regularly changing specials. When children come in famished from the garden they will be pleased to find their own menu (mums and dads will be equally delighted by the pricing).

The opening hours are from 11 am to 3 pm and 6 pm to 11 pm on weekdays, with all day opening (11 am to 11 pm) on Saturday. On Sunday the Bell opens from noon to 3 pm and 7 pm to 10.30 pm. Food is served at lunchtime from noon to 2.30 pm every day. In the evening it is available from 6 pm to 9.30 pm, except on Sunday, when it is only on offer in summer, from 7 pm to 9 pm.

Telephone: 01432 760395.

How to get there: Tillington can be reached from the A4110, which joins the A438 Hereford to Brecon road at the White Cross roundabout. Go to the west off the A4110 at the Starting Gate roundabout, then turn quickly right at the traffic lights. Follow this road, passing St Mary's Hospital and ignoring the turnings for Burghill, and after about 3 miles the Bell Inn will appear on the right.

Parking: There is a large car park to the rear of the inn.

Length of the walk: 3½ miles. Map: OS Landranger 149 Hereford, Leominster and surrounding area (inn GR 464454).

Blossom time in May is a particularly lovely time to do this walk, alternatively through the soft fruit season or at apple harvest in autumn – it's difficult to go wrong! The route takes you on paths through cider orchards to the pretty setting of Burghill church. From here a steady climb earns views over central Herefordshire. The descent is through a farm, so in season there is an opportunity to bear home the fruits of your efforts.

The Walk

From the Bell Inn car park take the minor road leading from the junction across the front of the pub. At the next junction go right, and then left along the access road to (Tillington) Court Farm. A stile on the right invites you across a field to the far right-hand corner, where you go over the fence/stile facing you – not the more obvious stile to the right. Keep the field edge on your right as you

54

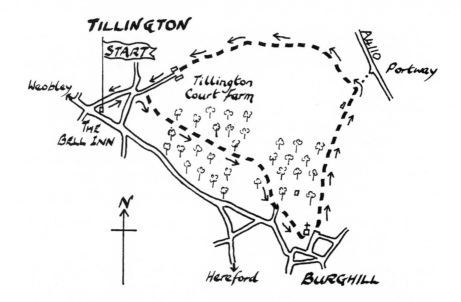

enter the apple orchards. You will soon pick up a metalled track –
follow this to the left.

Cider has been a popular drink in this area for many centuries,
probably since before the Romans arrived. It went through periods
of national popularity, but declined during the 19th century.
Despite this, most farmhouses would have had their own cider
press in use. It was Percy Bulmer, the son of the rector of nearby
Credenhill, who rescued the industry and brought it back to
countrywide significance. The company he founded still prospers in
Hereford and, nearby, there is the Cider Museum.

The track curves left, then right (at a waymark post). On your
right the path is flanked by tall poplars, guarding the apple trees
against strong winds. It now bends to the right. On the next bend is
a waymark post, on the right. This is the signal to leave the track
along a path to the right. Cross a stile and briefly go left on a tarmac
access road.

Take your time over the route-finding here. A waymark post
guides you to the left and through a gate, back into the orchards.
On reaching another track, go right. At the next waymark post head
diagonally off on the left, crossing the lines of trees. A kissing-gate
will bring you into the churchyard of St Mary at Burghill.

The church itself was heavily restored in 1880, but the stem and rim of the lead bowl of the font date from around 1200. There are effigies of around 1440 and a brass memorial to Robert Masters, traveller, who died in 1619. The composer Edward Elgar used to cycle here, and sketched the font. Dorothy Wordsworth married the owner of nearby Brinsop Court, and her brother William stood in the hollow tree in the churchyard with Coleridge and Southey.

With your back to the porch, turn left. The path takes you out of the churchyard, onto a lane. Go left. Now comes a steady climb. Upon reaching the summit of the lane there are rewarding views over the gentle valley of the river Lugg, the wooded hills of Badnage and Dinmore, and beyond.

Start the descent, but on the way down a bridleway sign on the left marks the gate you should pass through. Initially keep the woodland edge on your left, through a gate, but then lose height fairly quickly as you go forward. There is no path underfoot but you will come to a gate in the fence ahead, with the main road a little distance at your back.

After passing through this gate, another one beckons ahead, but instead go over a stile in the field corner, to its right. Bear left, past a pool and onto a track. This will lead you through the buildings of Tillington Court Farm, onto tarmac, and so to the road. Turn right, then left, to return to the Bell Inn.

Places of interest nearby
After all those orchards you must visit the *Cider Museum and King Offa Cider Brandy Distillery* off the Whitecross Road in Hereford. Displays illustrate the cider-making process, ancient and modern, including an old farm cider house. If this makes you thirsty, there is an off-licence. Opening hours are restricted during the winter, so please phone ahead to check (01432 54207).

12

Hereford — King's Acre Road
The Bay Horse

Hereford is indeed a fortunate city, with an attractive historic core and surrounded by lovely scenery. It is very easy, however, to whizz along the Brecon road, out into countryside, without stopping to appreciate the beauty on the doorstep.

The Bay Horse Inn, about 2 miles from the city centre, is a Whitbread partnership house and has been refurbished to a high standard. The country house style interior of stained wood and pretty decor conveys a warm and cosy atmosphere in which to contemplate the choice of Flowers Original and Best, Bass and Boddingtons bitters, or Murphy's Stout and Heineken and Stella Artois lagers. Local cider makers Bulmer are well represented by their Original, Strongbow, GL and Scrumpy Jack brews and the wine list features a range of New World wines. The menu is equally cosmopolitan – steaks, Philly Cheesesteak and steak and ale pie are joined by traditional North American and Mexican dishes such as nachos, frito misto and steak fajita. There are Thai and oriental dishes, and vegetarian and vegan options. Children have their own selection and, where feasible, senior citizens can have half portions of the regular menu at half price. All of this excellent fare is, surprisingly, home-made. There is a lovely garden room/ conservatory to soak up the sun, even on cooler days, and a pleasant beer garden. Children's games can be requested at the bar.

The hours are easily remembered – noon until 3 pm each day, with evening opening from 5.30 pm on weekdays, 6 pm on Saturday and 7 pm on Sunday, in each case until 11 pm. Food is available from noon until 2 pm each day and from 6 pm to 9.30 pm on weekdays. On Saturday it is served in the evening from 6 pm to 10 pm, and from 7 pm to 9 pm on Sunday.

Telephone: 01432 273351.

How to get there: The Bay Horse is situated on the A438 Hereford to Brecon road, about ¾ mile west of the White Cross roundabout, its intersection with the A4110.

Parking: There is a car park to the side of the inn.

Length of the walk: 4¼ miles. Map: OS Landranger 149, Hereford, Leominster and surrounding area (inn GR 478412).

This walk takes you over fields to the National Trust beauty spot of Breinton Springs. From here, company is first kept with the idyllic river Wye, before returning along very quiet country lanes and paths.

The Walk
Facing the inn is a bridleway sign, clearly indicating the direction to be taken. Keeping the side of the field to your right, pass through a gate and continue to a gate on the right. Go through this, proceeding along the lane at right angles to your original direction. After passing a few houses, the track becomes a path and enters woodland.

Just as you leave the trees there is a waymarked stile on your left. Go over this and again keep the hedge to your right, over a stile, through a gateway and so to a road. Cross over and another stile gives access to a field, this time with the hedge to your left. Pass through a gate, then the next one leads into an orchard, now with the hedge to the right.

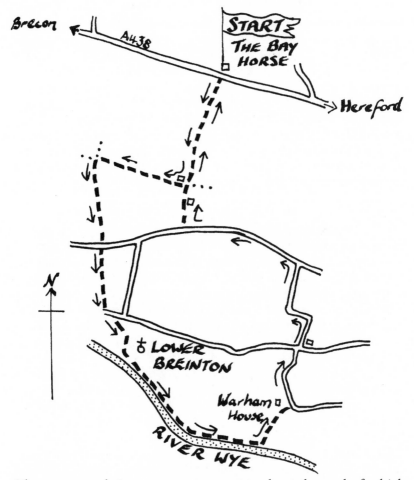

The next gate brings you to a grassy track, at the end of which you go through the facing pedestrian gate. Cross the orchard diagonally to the kissing-gate in the far left corner. Once through, go right to enter Breinton Springs, owned by the National Trust. This is the site of a deserted medieval village and an information board explains about the excavation of a manor house.

Follow the path down to the river bank. If you then detour to the right you will see one of the springs. The Wye has here gouged a way through glacial deposits.

Returning to the main path, now continue along the river bank. You may well meet many fellow walkers, for this is part of the Wye

Valley Walk, which runs from Chepstow, through Ross to Hereford, and so to Hay-on-Wye and on to Rhayader in Wales. It is a delectable route, with scarcely a dull moment. Even if you cannot complete it all in one holiday, it is still worth undertaking in day walks.

Also along here are joggers, fishermen on the riverbank, rowers on the water and golfers on the opposite side of the river. All-in-all, a recreational haven for Herefordians. It would be easy to go with the flow all the way back to the city centre, but instead take a stile to the left, just before the second footbridge. Bear right, following the stream, passing in front of the distinguished red brick of Warham House.

At the road go left, then at a junction turn right and immediately left. This road is so little used that it does not even merit a sign and has grass growing up the middle. At the next junction go left.

At the entrance to Little Breinton there are some relics of cider-making days. The cider mill comprises a round stone with a groove in it (the runner) and another round stone set on edge (the chase) which is seated in the groove. Into the groove were poured apples and the chase was pulled around, generally by a horse or perhaps an ox. The mill could not remove all the juice from the apples, although it did produce 110 gallons per day. The remaining pulp was wrapped in cloths and eight or ten of these parcels ('cheeses') were stacked on top of each other. They were placed in the other device on show, the press, which was screwed down to release the remaining juice. Even the dry pulp was not wasted, being fed to pigs.

Turn right at the bridleway sign, passing Upper Hill Farm. At a sharp bend go through the gate on your right. Once through, turn immediately left, having now rejoined the outward route. The Bay Horse will be in sight ahead.

Places of interest nearby
The Weir, further west along the A438. National Trust gardens featuring spring bulbs, autumn acacias and colours, set on the banks of the Wye. *The Waterworks Museum* at Broomy Hill in Hereford has working displays of steam and other engines, pumps (including some that visitors can use), a horse-drawn fire engine and so on. Check opening times with the Tourist Information Centre (01432 268430).

⑬ Madley
The Red Lion

Some believe that Madley means 'the good place', and few would deny that the description still fits today. The Romans built a road nearby and in the Middle Ages this was a place of pilgrimage. Nowadays the fascinating white dishes of the Madley Communications Centre never seem far away.

The Red Lion is at the heart of the village – and has its own slice of history. Dating back to the 11th century in parts, and originally a farm, it became a coaching inn during the 15th century. The ghost of a Cavalier from the Civil War lurks downstairs and he likes to mess around with the gas in the cellar.

The public bar retains its stone-flagged floor and there is a dartboard and pool table to entertain you. The lounge is snugly carpeted. On offer are Burton Ale and the local Wye Valley Bitter, as well as Skol and Carlsberg lagers. Other local brews are GL and Scrumpy Jack ciders. Wine aficionados can choose between the house wines, muscadet and claret. The food is home-made and includes traditional favourites such as ham and eggs, casseroles and steak and kidney pie, and a very popular Sunday lunch. Children have their own part of the menu, with chicken nuggets, beefburgers and sausages and so on. An additional thoughtful touch is that child portions of other dishes are available. At the side of the inn is a beer garden with play equipment, an ideal family location for lazy summer afternoons and evenings.

The inn opens at noon each day, to 2.30 pm from Tuesday to Friday (closed Monday lunchtime) and to 3 pm at weekends. Evening opening is 6.45 pm to 11 pm, except on Sunday, when it is 7 pm to 10.30 pm. Food is served from noon to 1.45 pm and 7 pm to 9.30 pm, except, again, Sunday evening, when only drinks are available.

Telephone: 01981 250292.

How to get there: Madley lies about 2 miles west of Clehonger on the B4352, which runs between the A465 south of Hereford and the B4348 outside Hay-on-Wye.

Parking: There is a car park to the rear of the inn, but please let someone know if you wish to leave your car there whilst you go walking.

Length of the walk: 3½ miles. Map: OS Landranger 149 Hereford, Leominster and surrounding area (inn GR 426384).

Opening with a little road walking, the route then heads over fields. It goes round the perimeter of the Earth Satellite Station, with quite close views of the array of receivers. More field paths then return you to the village, where there is an opportunity to view one of the most impressive churches in the county.

The Walk

Turn left on leaving the inn, and at the junction go right, passing the church on your left. On the outskirts of the village is a chapel which, even in these parts, is unusual because it is half-timbered. Shortly afterwards there is a footpath sign on the left, at a stile opposite Blenheim Farm.

Cross the stile and initially keep the hedge on your left. Where it bends more sharply to the left go half-right to a stile and a footbridge. Keep ahead to arrive at a track and go left.

Look for a footpath sign and a stile on the right, just before The

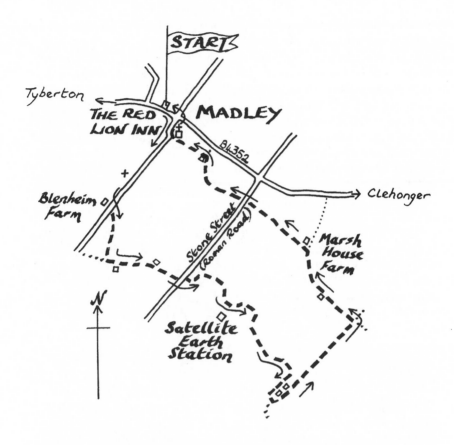

Hale. Over the stile, keep the field side on your left to the road. This is the Roman road known as Stone Street. Briefly go left and on the right is another footpath sign and a stile to be traversed. This path soon bends left and now follows the perimeter fence of the satellite station.

Opened in 1978, there are now 11 dishes tracking telecommunications satellites 36,000 km above the earth. This is one of only 2 such centres in the UK, the other being at Goonhilly Downs in Cornwall. There are also 2 international telephone exchanges here, each capable of 500,000 call attempts per hour. The sheer scale of the technology cannot fail to impress, ranging from the 7 reserve generators capable of producing up to 6 megawatts of electricity to the transmitters which emit communications sequences in 2 millisecond bursts. And all this in the quiet heart of Herefordshire.

The path takes a 90° right turn and passes to the rear of some houses, before coming out onto a track. Go left, in front of the houses, down to the left corner of the field. Pass through the facing gate (not the one to the left) to enter a large field. Go straight across, to the bottom. As you do so, the hedge on the right drifts away and then comes closer. At the end of the field is a stream. Do not be tempted across the footbridge, but turn to the left and make for the track to the right of the farm buildings.

Follow the track past a poultry farm. Go through a gate on the left immediately before a new barn, then walk just right of straight ahead to a waymarked gate. Cross an orchard to another gate. Bear slightly right to a stiled footbridge, then keep ahead to the road.

Cross the road and go through a gate next to a footpath sign. Climb the stile ahead, then keep the hedge to your left. A couple more stiles will bring you to a lane, where you go right. Turn left at a footpath sign, initially just inside the garden of a house, to a stile. Now the side of the field is on the right. A narrow hedged path will

Madley church.

bring you to a kissing-gate into the churchyard. This is Madley parish church, the Nativity of the Virgin.

Nothing remains of the original wooden church, probably founded by St Dyfrig or Dubricius around AD 550. Much of the existing building dates from the 13th century, and the Norman font is one of the largest in Britain. Other ancient remnants are the early 14th-century wall paintings above the chancel arch and the stained glass in the top half of the middle window, which dates from as early as 1250. The overriding impression is of a very large church for a small village – why? Well, it seems that this was a place of pilgrimage, probably because of the presence of a statue of the Virgin Mary, which was believed to have special powers. This probably also accounts for the unusual dedication of the church.

Leave the churchyard by going half-left from the porch to the gate at the corner by the junction. Continue along the main street to return to the Red Lion.

Places of interest nearby

To the west along the B4352 is the village of *Bredwardine*, where the Reverend Francis Kilvert lived. His countryside diaries are still widely read today. *Brobury House*, just outside Bredwardine, has a marvellous art gallery (take your chequebook) and super gardens.

14 Peterchurch
The Boughton Arms

Peterchurch lies deep in the Golden Valley, a name that perhaps conjures up visions of cornfields burnished by a giant sun. In high summer it can be like that, but there are also pastures in the bottom of this gentle dip, and woods on its slopes.

The Boughton Arms assumes a prominent position on the road through the village. White-painted, it offers a large and delightfully unpretentious public bar, a place for locals and walkers to exchange banter or to play pool and darts. There is also a comfy lounge leading to a suntrap patio beer garden. Why the inn is so named is a minor mystery, although a Sir Richard Boughton did have a hunting lodge at nearby Poston. Once upon a time there was a cock pit here, well patronised by supporters of that cruel sport – but that was 200 years ago.

A goodly selection of beers is on offer, including Whitbread Best, Welsh Bitter and Hereford Traditional. Heineken and Stella Artois lagers and Stowford Press ciders are other thirst-quenchers, along with a number of red and white wines. The pub prides itself on the splendid range of 60 meals and snacks. The sandwiches are amongst the most substantial to be found anywhere and more varied cuisine includes stuffed pitta bread, seafood Mornay, trout with jacket potato and steaks. Children are welcome both inside and out.

The pub opens from 11 am to 3 pm and 6 pm to 11 pm on Monday to Friday, meals being available from noon to 2 pm and 6 pm to 9 pm. On Saturday it is open from 11 am to 11 pm, with meals served from noon to 9 pm. Sunday opening hours are as Saturday in season, but check in advance at other times of the year. Telephone: 01981 550208.

How to get there: Peterchurch lies on the B4348, which runs between Hay-on-Wye and the A465 south of Hereford.

Parking: There is a large car park to the rear of the pub.

Length of the walk: 3¼ miles. Map: OS Landranger 149 Hereford, Leominster and surrounding area (inn GR 345385).

There is an opportunity to explore Peterchurch's charming church, then paths and quiet roads lead to a lane climbing, at a steady gradient, partway up the valley side. On paths again, you walk through woodland and a pleasant upland vale, and past a legendary spring, on your way back to the village street.

The Walk
From the pub car park walk around to Station Road, which leads off the main road to the front of the pub. In the angle of the junction is the entrance to the churchyard – go through this, to the church.

Consider the contrast between the remains of the 8th-century stonework in the apse and the fibreglass spire erected in 1972. The majority of the church is Norman, as is the font, and the altar is a charmingly simple survivor of ancient Saxon times. On the south wall of the nave is a fish in a frame. This is an image of the immortal trout which St Peter placed in the Golden Well in nearby Dorstone.

On returning to the churchyard have a look at the trees. The usual venerable yew (about 700 years old) is joined by exotic youngsters, Wellingtonia and Himalayan pines.

Leave the churchyard by the main gate and go left, crossing the

67

river Dore. Some 100 years ago you could have boarded the Golden Valley train here, at Peterchurch station. The line ran 19 miles from Pontrilas to Hay-on-Wye, the journey taking one and half hours. In 1884 the railway carried 20,000 passengers and 4,000 tons of freight, but the line closed in 1951. On one occasion, in the days of the Great Western Railway, the church tower and spire were covered in scaffolding and an engine driver took a bet that he could climb to the top whilst his train was in the station – I wonder what his passengers thought!

Just over the bridge a tarmac path goes off to the left, then loops back and curves to join a lane by Hinton Farm. The lane leads to a minor road, where you go right. Turn right at a crossroads. You will shortly come to the main road (by the Nag's Head Inn, if you are already thirsty). Otherwise cross the main road and head up the lane to Mowbage Farm.

The lane climbs steadily until you reach Greenway Farm. Here take the track forking off to the right, passing some modern barns. After a sharp left bend you will be faced by a gate. Turn right and the track takes you to a pedestrian gate into woodland. A path leads off to the right, moving close to the woodland edge.

You will soon leave the wood by another pedestrian gate. Continue left, still following the edge of the wood. A field gate between two belts of woodland opens out views of an upland valley. Initially, keep high on the right side of the valley, detouring past some Dutch barns.

The route now joins a lane which can be very muddy as it follows a small stream. At a junction, with a house on your right, you should hear the sound of gushing water. You are at the site of St Peter's Well, regrettably overgrown at the time of writing. As a result, little can be seen of the carved stone head from which the water flows.

Once the well fed a bathing pool which was said to cure rheumatism, and pins thrown into holes in the well wall cured eye problems.

Continue down the lane (not the access road). When you come to a red-brick house (The Cottage) on your right, take the lane leading downhill to your left. There are views out over the church spire to the Hatterall Ridge on the Welsh border. Pass Bazley Farm on your way back to the village. Once you arrive at the main road go right to return to the Boughton Arms.

Places of interest nearby
To the north is Dorstone, above which, on the hills but at the roadside, is the megalithic tomb known as *Arthur's Stone*. The capstone is estimated to weight 25 tons. To the south, via the B4347, are *Abbey Dore Court Gardens*, set out on the banks of the river. There are herbaceous borders, tall Wellingtonias, rockpools and a plant sales centre.

⑮ Aston Crews
The Ha'penny

East of Ross-on-Wye is rolling countryside, continuing the landscape of the Forest of Dean but with less tree cover. Further east, just over the Gloucestershire border near Newent and Dymock there are more large woodlands. Here in Herefordshire the views are open, with the conifer-capped crown of May Hill almost always near at hand. Aston Crews is one of the quiet hamlets to be found along some of the twisting byways, and it occupies a hilltop position that allows one to survey the surrounding countryside. It has not one but two good pubs and is a popular short outing for Ross folk.

You may be quite surprised when you open the door of the Ha'penny, previously the White Hart. Here, perched on a Herefordshire hill, miles from the sea – or even the river Wye – is a nautically-themed pub, with multi-coloured ship's lanterns and a mini-grotto surmounted by an anchor catching your eye. The small rooms have been opened out, but quiet corners are created by dividers of oars or ship's wheels. In amongst all this, and the

70

drawings and models of ships, are horse brasses, harnesses and other country paraphernalia, and a big fireplace with a basket grate. There is also a separate poolroom. Outside, the lovely long-distance views from the patio will take your breath away.

The large, central bar is very accessible amid all the accessories, and you will be reassured to find Banks's and Marston's Bitters and Wadworth 6X on draught. Other brews include John Smith's Bitter, Murphy's Stout, and Stella Artois and Heineken lagers. Strongbow and GL ciders are also on offer. The inn was renamed to emphasise that it has a sister pub, the Pennyfarthing, just around the corner. Whereas the Pennyfarthing serves à la carte restaurant meals, the Ha'penny provides good value bar snacks – scampi and chips, steak and kidney pie and the usual sandwiches, soup and ploughman's lunches. Children's needs are not forgotten, with infallible favourites such as fish fingers or sausages and chips waiting for them.

At the time of writing the inn was closed on weekday lunchtimes. It opens from noon to 3 pm at weekends and every night from 6 pm (7 pm in winter) to 11 pm. Food is served from noon to 2 pm at weekends and from 6.30 pm (7.30 pm in winter) to 9 pm.

Telephone: 01989 750203.

How to get there: Aston Crews lies north of the A40 between Ross-on-Wye and Gloucester. Turn off on the B4222 just west of the Crown Inn in Lea. On reaching the village, go left at the top of the hill and the Ha'penny is just on the left.

Parking: There is a large car park at the side of the inn and extra parking facing it.

Length of the walk: 3 miles. Map: OS Landranger 162, Gloucester and Forest of Dean area (inn GR 671233).

This walk takes you via some quiet field paths to the hamlet of Aston Ingham, where the church sits in a very pretty spot. From here more paths and a little road walking take you up hill and down dale. There are ample excuses to rest on the little hilltops and to take in views stretching round from nearby May Hill to the Malverns and still further to the eminences of South Wales.

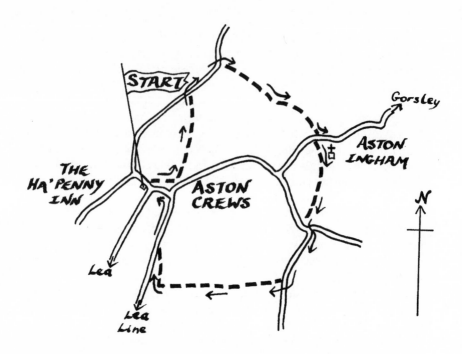

The Walk

Cross the road from the inn. Go over a stile in the parking bay fence
and keep the field side to your right. At the bottom of the field cross
a stile and go left. At the bottom of this field there is a plank
footbridge skulking amongst the bushes, followed by a stile. Once
over the stile, climb the hill towards a bungalow. This will bring you
to a gate onto a road, where you turn right.

Pass a farm and go through a gate on the right at a footpath sign.
Another gate quickly follows. Cross the field diagonally right to a
gate in the bottom corner. It can be quite muddy here. Now keep to
the left of the field you have just entered and pass through one
more gate on the way to the road. You are now in Aston Ingham.

To the left is the church of St John the Baptist, by a small, typically
English village green. The church was largely rebuilt in the 19th
century, but inside is a very rare lead font of 1689, decorated with
foliage and the initials of William and Mary, and 13th-century
effigies are set on either side of the altar. An interesting time to be
here is the nearest Sunday to Candlemas Day (2nd February), when
small loaves known as Garrold's Bread are blessed and handed out

to parishioners. This custom is not as ancient as it may seem, as it dates from an 1859 bequest.

If you believe the theories of Herefordian Alfred Watkins, who wrote in 1925, you are in a location of some significance. While he was a successful businessman and pioneer photographer of historic buildings, he is best known for his controversial publications on ley lines, linking many prehistoric sites. He believed one such line, from May Hill to Aconbury camp near Hereford, ran through here.

No straight lines for us. On leaving the church turn left along the road and over a stream. Go through a gate on the left at a footpath sign. Keep towards, but not right up to, the left-hand hedge. A gate leads onto a road, where you go left. Once around the corner and past a farm on the right, cross a stiled footbridge on the right and climb the slope ahead.

Go over the stile at the top of the hill, then the one immediately on the left. Go right. You may wish to pause here, to look back at May Hill. The tuft of Scots pines on its summit locates it from miles around. To the right as you continue, the range of the Malvern Hills disappears into the distance.

The hedge is now to your right as you cross another stile and descend into a valley. One more stile and a plank footbridge have to be negotiated. Go through a gateway in the valley bottom and climb another slope. This time the stile ahead leads onto a track.

Go right to join the road and at a junction turn left. Pass the Pennyfarthing Inn and at the next junction go right to the Ha'penny – I hope you won't feel short-changed by the exertions of this walk!

Places of interest nearby

At Clifford's Mesne, on the way to Newent, is the *National Birds of Prey Centre*, the largest private collection of birds of prey in Europe (open February to November). In Newent itself is *The Shambles*, a museum of shops and cottages as they were in Victorian times (open mid-March to December).

16 Weston-under-Penyard
The Weston Cross Inn

Weston sits in the shadow of Penyard Hill, on the Gloucester side of Ross-on-Wye, a village that people often drive through without being aware of what might lie in store if they just took the time to explore. The Weston Cross Inn is placed conspicuously enough to tempt some to stop, and those who do will be well rewarded. Its solid local sandstone may be rapidly vanishing under a creeper disguise, but it has no reason to be shy.

The front of the inn is home to the bar and the pool table. Stroll along the corridor to the lounge and you have to pass the kitchen, enough to whet anyone's appetite. The lounge itself is clearly a place for serious eating, with well-spaced tables and a thick carpet. If you prefer something natural underfoot – and if the weather permits – there are picnic tables out in the beer garden. Here also is a friendly giant, whose outstretched arms welcome children on to the swings.

Returning to the bar, you will find Flowers Original and IPA, Boddingtons and Whitbread Best, alongside Murphy's Stout,

Heineken lager and Blackthorn and GL ciders. As for food, starters include breaded whitebait and mushrooms with garlic dip. After that, there is considerable choice of main course. If you fancy fish, the seafood platter might be a tempting proposition. Meat dishes include steaks, curries, chilli and sizzling Cajun chicken with rice. The jumbo rolls are pretty good value, as are Sunday lunches (for which booking is advised). Sweets are definitely in the traditional vein – in other words, filling. Childhood favourites for some of us, like jam roly poly or spotted dick, can be affectionately revisited. Today's children wil be delighted to learn that they have their own section of the menu, and don't the chicken teddies sound too good to eat!

Opening hours on Monday to Saturday run from 11.45 am to 3 pm and 7 pm to 11 pm, whilst the times on Sunday are noon to 3 pm and 7 pm to 10.30 pm. Food is served from noon to 2 pm and from 7 pm to 9 pm every day, so that's easy to remember.

Telephone: 01989 562759.

How to get there: Weston-under-Penyard lies a couple of miles east of Ross, on the A40 road to Gloucester. The Weston Cross Inn is situated on the main road, which goes through the village.

Parking: There is a large car park to the side of the inn.

Length of the walk: 2½ miles. Map: OS Landranger 162 Gloucester and Forest of Dean area (inn GR 631234).

Weston, like so many Herefordshire villages, has a history going back to at least Roman times. After all, Ariconium, the site of many archaeological finds, is just east of here. However, I have to confess that the castle we pass is a fake, but no less interesting for that. The views on the walk are good, extending to the Welsh borders and the Malvern Hills.

The Walk

On emerging from the inn, or its car park, turn left. At a footpath sign go left, passing between garden hedges and over a stile. Next, pass right along a row of stables, no doubt with the resident horses inspecting your appearance. Go through a gate and bear half-right to a stile. Once over, continue along the longest axis of the field to

75

another stile and some steps down. If the gardens on your left appear to contain some strange objects, it is because they belong to a training centre. I'm not bright enough to understand how they are used.

Carry on across the field you have just entered, then two more stiles will take you across a track. Now bear a little to the right over this small field and a stile and some steps will take you down to a minor road. Go left. Just past a modern bungalow there is a gate on the right and a stile to be crossed. Follow the track uphill, but at the top of the rise go briefly right to find a stile which will take you into an orchard.

Keep the hedge to your left. Further afield are views over Ross church and to Skirrid Fawr near Abergavenny. The orchard ends, but continue alongside a field to enter another orchard. At a waymark post another path crosses our route. A little further on, look out for a stile in the hedge on the left (easily missed). Cross this one and go right, to a stile and a minor road. Go right.

Just past the council houses there is a stone tower on the left. This used to be a dovecote, in the days when these birds were kept for their edible qualities (and their eggs). Now it houses a water tank.

Bollitree Castle.

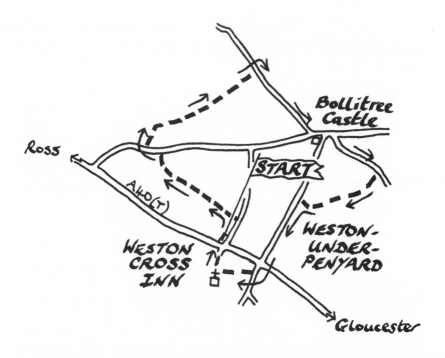

Soon you will be faced at a junction by Bollitree Castle. The house itself is a pleasant enough mid-17th-century red sandstone building, but as you bear to the left there is a moat, defending battlements.

This daunting frontage only protects farm buildings and is, in fact, a 17th-century 'Gothick' confection. Parts came from Penyard Castle, on the hill behind Weston, and others from a Bristol church – no doubt brought up the Wye as far as Ross. Was this simply an aesthetic project, like the later imitation town walls in Ross itself? We do not know for sure, but there are a couple of romantic stories about the castle.

It is said that the walls were built because the beautiful girl Thomas Hopkins, the landowner, fell in love with longed to live in a castle. Another version is that he was betrothed to a Spanish princess who would live in nothing but a castle. Needless to say, when she saw his attempts she was not deceived and she rapidly vanished. Fanciful though these stories may seem, Thomas' ghost perambulates the lawns of the castle, we are told, and that of a lady ascends the stairs.

Pass the battlements and take the second road to the right (off which the track to Bollitree Farm leads). Continue down the minor road and go over a stile on the right. Head just to the left of the large house to be seen over the field. You are here quite close to the Roman settlement of Ariconium, believed to have been the major smelting centre for iron ore from the Forest of Dean. Furnaces have been excavated and many artefacts, such as bronze brooches, but particularly coins (once known as fairies' money), have been found.

After you have crossed the field another stile is followed quickly by a gate as the path leads through a small plantation. From the next gate continue, with the hedge on your left, to a pedestrian gate and so to the road. The building you saw to the right is the 17th-century Old Rectory, complete with pedimented doorway, but we are going left.

A bridge takes you over the abandoned Ross to Gloucester railway. Built to broad gauge standards in 1855, it closed in 1975. Cross the main road and go along the minor road, signed for the village hall and sports field. Turn right, just before the school, towards the church of St Lawrence. The porch dates from the 14th or 15th century. The nave has an arcade of Norman arches and the carvings of forest beasts upon them are a particularly nice feature. Have a look at the middle window on the north wall of the chancel, where there is a carving of a beast eating a man.

On leaving via the porch, go through the gate ahead and down the path to a lane. Go right to return to the main road, the other side of which is the Weston Cross Inn.

Places of interest nearby
Ross-on-Wye, with its shops, lovely riverside walks and the Lost Street and Button Museums, is barely 3 miles away.

⑰ Sellack
The Lough Pool Inn

Set in an idyllic spot near the delightful hamlet of Sellack and the river Wye, the Lough Pool Inn almost epitomises the Herefordshire country pub. It has some 17th-century half-timbering and is set behind an attractive beer garden off a road going nowhere in particular. The ancient cider press in the beer garden is a reminder of the days when most farmhouses would have made their own cider.

Inside, the stone-flagged floors and beamed ceilings (and, in winter, the added attraction of an open fire) combine to give a timeless feel – and the ghost is not to be feared. Food is a definite speciality and you can eat in the long bar with cosy corners off it, or the large dining room. You could start with the familiar soup and a roll or jumbo sausage and chips. On the other hand you could impress your friends later by describing the shark steak or wild boar casserole. The largely home-prepared food also includes Greek-style goat casserole, chicken korma and salmon steak in white wine sauce, plus 4 or 5 vegetarian dishes. The beers available include

Wye Valley Bitter, John Smith's and Bass, together with Stowford Press and Scrumpy Jack ciders. There is an excellent selection of wines.

The inn is open at lunchtime from 11.30 am to 3 pm on Monday to Saturday and from noon to 2.30 pm on Sunday. Evening hours are 6 pm to 11 pm on Monday to Saturday and 7 pm to 10.30 pm on Sunday. Food is served from noon to 2 pm and 7 pm to 9.30 pm, 9 pm on Sunday.

Telephone: 01989 730236.

How to get there: Sellack can be reached from the A49 between Hereford and Ross-on-Wye. Turn northwards on a minor road at the side of the Red Lion at Winter's Cross. Bear left at two forks and the Lough Pool Inn will appear on your right at a T-junction.

Parking: The inn has a large car park. You may leave your car here if you are a customer, but please let the staff know.

Length of the walk: 2½ miles. Map: OS Landranger 162 Gloucester and Forest of Dean area (inn GR 557268).

This is an easy, short walk with an initial stretch of road followed by a good track taking you to Sellack church and its many curiosities. From here you stroll briefly by the river Wye before returning via gentle valley pastures and woodland.

The Walk

From the inn car park entrance turn left along the road to Hoarwithy. This is canopied by lovely oak trees, but can be somewhat busy at weekends. There is a gradual climb to Caradoc Hill, giving views of the local countryside.

At the summit turn right, signed 'Caradoc – Private Road'. If in doubt, you will also see a seat, postbox, bus stop, bridleway signs and a clump of Scots pines at this point. This roadway passes Caradoc Farm with its stable complex. Then, on the left, there is Caradoc Court itself. The name is taken from the ancient British camp nearby and there could be connections with the eponymous hero of the resistance to the Romans – he was certainly in action locally. Tradition also links it to Sir Cradoc Vraich-vras (Strong Arm), one of the Knights of the Round Table.

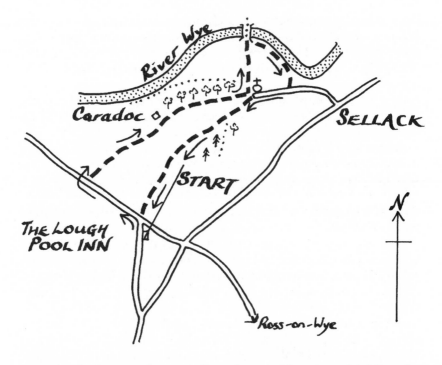

Much of what can be seen from here is Victorian, shielding the 16th-century black and white and 17th-century stone origins of the building. This area seems popular with birds and you may see a nuthatch patrolling the trees.

Carry on down the track, which descends to the red sandstone church of St Tysilio at Sellack. This is the only English dedication to this 7th-century saint. He was born in Shrewsbury, son of the King of Powys, and became a monk, for which he was persecuted by his royal relatives. Eventually, he escaped to establish a monastery in Brittany, at what is now St Suliac, the French Sellack.

The church we see today has 12th-century origins, but has been much altered and extended over the centuries. The east window is a treasure, with 14th-century tracery and an amalgam of stained glass from the 14th, 15th and 16th centuries, all pieced together in 1630. The pulpit and some of the other woodwork is 17th century. There is a continuous record of ministers from 1291.

A handout in the church describes a Civil War incident. Parliamentary soldiers visited the village with the intention of

81

destroying the churchyard cross and the chancel window. The vicar received them very hospitably, so as to distract them from their destructive intent. He succeeded, except in the case of one soldier, who satisfied his honour by firing his gun at the lower corner of the window.

One of the most intriguing features is to be found in the churchyard – a stone cross, sculpted with a finger pointing to the sky, and the succinct inscription, 'Gone'.

Return to the road and turn right, through a gate and over the pastures to the suspension bridge across the river Wye. The bridge was built in 1896 from the proceeds of public subscription. It replaced a ford and a ferry, although a former vicar is said to have used stilts to get to the other side. Don't cross over – this would take you to King's Caple. Instead, turn right, along the river bank. This curves round, and where scrub obstructs the route a path veers away up a gentle slope to the road. Turn right.

Just before arriving back at the church look for a footpath sign on the left. Cross the stile here and head along the bottom of this gentle valley.

A stile now leads into woodland – ignore a fainter path leading uphill. There is a good path by a tiny stream, shaded by some very tall ash trees. It is worth pausing, as you may well see the squirrels scampering about in the canopy. Another stile takes you back into grassland. Bear slightly right at the top of the slope for one more stile and then the road. The Lough Pool Inn is directly ahead.

Places of interest nearby
The unusual Italianate church at *Hoarwithy*, the next village. *How Caple Court*, north-east of King's Caple, with 11 acres of ornamental gardens, a church with delightful stained glass and a fabric shop and tea room.

18 Wilton
The Hereford Bull Inn

Wilton may now just seem to be a suburb of Ross-on-Wye, the site of a roundabout off the town's bypass, but it is a village with its own history. As an important crossing of the river Wye, it once boasted a ferry, long since replaced by the bridge we see today, and a castle to guard it.

The Hereford Bull Inn has stood on the banks of the river since around 1770. Its sturdy red sandstone also encompasses the old jail, which dates back to 1590 and which is now a restaurant. The main lounge displays plenty of that local stone, as well as an open fireplace, and is adorned with angling paraphernalia – hardly surprising, really. There is a skittle alley, too. The riverside garden is a lovely place to sit, especially when the mute swans glide by on warm summer evenings. If you would like to linger longer, then overnight accommodation is also available.

There is a full evening restaurant menu served from 6 pm to 9 pm daily. The bar food includes starters such as deep-fried wedges of Brie with cranberry sauce. Main courses range from the inevitable Bullburgers, through Hereford Steak, mushroom and stout pie, to chicken curry Madras with poppadoms. A blackboard displays the day's specials – when I was last there pancakes with prawns and mushrooms in cheese sauce made a particularly tasty dish. Sweets are no less attractive, for example sherry trifle cheesecake, would you believe? The usual children's favourites are also on offer. Liquid refreshments come in the form of Bass, Boddingtons and Wye Valley Bitters, also Gale's Pompey Royal, a beer less commonly found locally. Heineken and Stella Artois lagers and Scrumpy Jack cider are also served.

The inn opens from 11.30 am until 3 pm and again from 6 pm to 11 pm (10.30 pm on Sunday). Bar snacks are available from noon to 2 pm and from 7 pm to 9 pm.

Telephone: 01989 562785.

How to get there: The Hereford Bull Inn will be found just by the river, on the Ross side of the Wilton roundabout, which is the junction of the A49 Hereford road with the A40 Monmouth to Gloucester road. Take the turning beside the river, between the bridge and the roundabout, and the inn is almost immediately on the left.

Parking: There is a small car park to the rear of the inn and limited on-street parking. If all spaces are full, cross the bridge and there is a large pay-and-display car park to the right.

Length of the walk: 2½ miles. Map: OS Landranger 162 Gloucester and Forest of Dean area (inn GR 588242).

After crossing the ancient bridge over the Wye, we wander along the riverside. Our path then curves onto a low sandstone ridge, joining the Wye Valley Walk to enter Ross. There are superb views over the famous horseshoe bends of the river Wye, an ancient market house and tales of John Kyrle, the 'Man of Ross'. Descending to the riverside meadows, we catch glimpses of the ruined castle of Wilton.

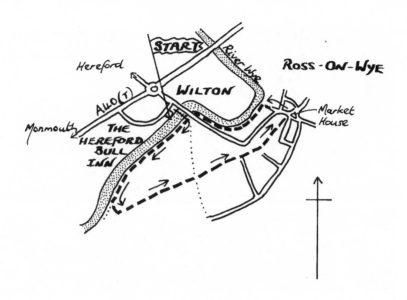

The Walk

Turn right on leaving the inn and at the main road go right again. There was once a ferry here, particularly remembered for a disaster during the reign of Elizabeth I in which 40 people died. The river has a reputation for demanding a quota of human lives, many being deceived by its tranquil appearance.

The bridge must have been very welcome when it opened in 1599. The prominent sundial was installed in the 18th century and I am told that the much-weathered inscription reads, 'Esteem this precious time, which pass so swift away. Prepare thee for eternity, and do not make delay'. We seem to have started the walk in philosophical mood, so now hasten over the bridge and go down the steps to the right.

Continue along the river bank, usually with hopeful fishermen just below the level of the path. Vegetation luxuriates along here during the summer, especially Himalayan balsam, or jumping jack, with its pink flowers. Glimpses of the river are likely to be rewarded by a sight of swans serenely floating up and down.

A Wye Valley Walk waymark post on the right indicates the point at which to leave the river bank, shortly before a stream crossing.

85

View from the Prospect.

Join a track to the left. This joins another track at a waymark post for a circular walk – go left here. At the next junction a couple of tracks cross over (by a footpath sign) to join a path climbing to the left of the sewage works (sorry, can't be avoided!). The works are soon left behind, and you will pass through a kissing-gate.

Walk along this low ridge. A stile and a kissing-gate follow, before you descend to a track cut through the rock and go up the steps at the other side. Kissing-gates are very popular here. After the next one go right at a signposted junction of paths, then quickly climb some steps on the left (signed for the John Kyrle Walk and the Wye Valley Walk).

After the next kissing-gate the Wye Valley Walk disappears to the right, but our walk continues ahead. On arriving at the churchyard, go right then left to arrive at the Prospect. Go through the gateway and walk to the edge to admire the views over the serpentine curves of the Wye. The Prospect was laid out by John Kyrle, a notable benefactor of the town. He lived here between 1660 and his death in 1724 and others of his many good works included bringing piped water into the town, paying for children to be educated and providing bread for the poor.

Return through the main gateway and turn left. You will pass the church of St Mary, well worth a look inside, particularly at the 15th-century stained glass figures in the east window and the alabaster Rudhall tomb. Outside, the Plague Cross is a reminder of the 315 souls who died in 1637.

Bear diagonally across the front of the church to Church Street, faced by the Rudhall Almshouses, which were rebuilt in 1575. Turn left and at the bottom of the street turn right to the red sandstone Market House of 1660. High on the east wall is a white medallion of Charles II. Opposite the Market House is the black and white house of John Kyrle.

Return along High Street, end on to the Market House. Pass the tourist information centre. Continue ahead down Wye Street and the steps at the end. Pass the side of the Hope and Anchor Inn and go left. Follow the riverside, here by playing fields where fairs and carnivals are held.

Go up to the steps onto Wilton bridge and cross over. To your right you should be able to glimpse amongst the trees the remains of Wilton Castle. It guarded the river crossing from the 12th century, but was burned down by Parliamentarian forces during the Civil War. Once over the bridge turn left to return to the inn.

Places of interest nearby

The Lost Street Museum is just off Brookend Street in Ross. It comprises a range of shops as they would have appeared at the turn of the century. The pub, the Lillie Langtry, was reconstructed from its origins in the East End of London. The *Button Museum*, in Kyrle Street is believed to be unique. On display are over 8,000 buttons of up to 200 years old.

⑲ Garway
The Garway Moon Inn

The gently rolling Herefordshire countryside is very apparent in the area of the Welsh border. Bigger hills, deeper valleys, smaller villages and narrower roads begin to impress themselves on the view as one approaches from the east. Amongst all this, the Moon Inn at Garway sits serenely, overlooking a tranquil common complete with cricket pitch.

Inside, beamed ceilings reinforce the feeling of history in this 16th-century building. Stone walls, both natural and painted, add to the welcoming air of an old country farmhouse. The accommodation includes a large, comfortable lounge (one-third of which is reserved for non-smokers) and a smaller bar with a pool table and board skittles. At the rear there is a pleasant beer garden, which contains a pets' corner in summer, with goats, rabbits and guinea pigs to entertain younger visitors.

It may take some time to choose a drink from the wide selection here. Real ales could typically include London Pride, Flowers IPA, Bass, Fremlins and Double Dragon. Stella and Heineken lagers,

Scrumpy Jack, Strongbow and Woodpecker ciders and Murphy's Stout are all present and correct, with a choice of wines also available. Food in substantial portions is on offer. Baguettes, for example, or curries and chillies to warm you up on cooler days. Keep an eye on the specials board for less usual dishes, such as trout in sherry and Stilton sauce. Youngsters are not forgotten and will find chicken nuggets or fish fingers with chips, among other favourites. There is even a take-away service.

The pub is open from noon to 3 pm (2.30 pm on winter weekdays) and from 7 pm to 11 pm, except on Sunday, when it opens from noon to 3 pm and 7 pm to 10.30 pm. Food is served from noon to 2 pm and from 7 pm to 9.30 pm (to 10 pm on Saturdays and to 9 pm on Sunday).

Telephone: 01600 750270.

How to get there: Garway can be reached from the B4521 between its intersection with the A466 Hereford to Monmouth road and Skenfrith. Turn northwards at Broad Oak and the Moon Inn stands on the right about 1½ miles along this road.

Parking: There is an adequate car park to the front of the pub.

Length of the walk: 2¾ miles. Map: OS Landranger 161 Abergavenny and the Black Mountains (inn GR 465227).

The walk explores some of this remote border country, with lovely views over the Monnow valley to the rough hills of Wales. There is a detour to the ancient church of the Knights Templars and the adjoining medieval dovecote. The route is over field paths and on quiet byways.

The Walk
Turn left on leaving the pub car park. At the telephone box turn right down the road signed to Skenfrith. At the point where this road takes a sharp left bend go through the gate ahead (Dingle Lodge). Keep close to the hedge on your left as you pass the front of the house and you will come to a gate into a field.

Keep to the left as you walk down the field. At the bottom a gap in the hedge allows access to the road. Go right. From here there are lovely views over the valley of the river Monnow and to the hill

89

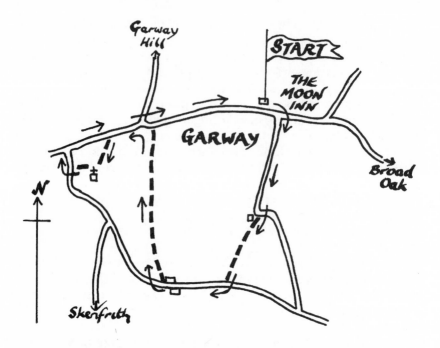

country of South Wales.

You will pass between the buildings of Garway Court. Just beyond them cross the rough stile in the hedge on the right and head up the field. Two gates in front offer a choice – take the right-hand one, immediately after crossing a streamlet. This path climbs, shaded by trees, on the edge of a gentle escarpment. You will soon be able to see Garway church at the base of the slope.

Go through a couple of gates to find the road and turn left. passing a junction. Look for a kissing-gate on the left. Go through and you should be able to see the church tower, so judge the line to take from this (about 45° to the road). There is another kissing-gate in the top corner of the churchyard.

This site was likely to have been chosen because of the existence of a spring, known as the Holy Well, now in the bottom corner of the churchyard. There was probably a Saxon predecessor, but what makes this church special is its association with the Knights Templars. This order was originally founded to protect pilgrims to the Holy Land and, as a result, gifts were readily bestowed. Garway, and 2,000 acres around it, was one such preceptory, which would raise funds for the Knights' foreign work. In the 14th century the Templars fell out of favour, and their possessions were taken over by the Knights Hospitallers, until they in turn were dispossessed by Henry VIII. This church was begin in the 1180s. Outside the north wall can be seen the excavated foundations of the round nave, which emulated that of the Church of the Holy Sepulchre in Jerusalem. As you walk round the building you will note the odd angle of the tower to the rest of the church. It was originally detached, probably as a defensive measure at a time when border raids were prevalent. On the walls are various carved and incised symbols. See if you can spot a dragon and the Lamb of God. Inside, the chancel arch is a lovely example of Norman work. The altar stone is medieval and the oak benches are of the 16th century.

In the farmyard next to the church is one of the best examples of a medieval dovecote in the country. It was probably rebuilt in 1326, and there are 666 nesting spaces. Both the eggs and the birds themselves (particularly the young) would have been a welcome supplement to the Knights' diet. If you would like a closer look at the dovecote, please walk round and ask permission at Clayfield Bungalow.

Leave the churchyard by the main entrance, and on reaching the road turn right, uphill. At the top of the hill turn right at the junction, passing the old chapel. Go past the road leading to Bagwylldiart, one of many Welsh place-names in this part of Herefordshire. About ½ mile will bring you back to the Moon Inn.

Places of interest nearby
There is a ruined castle in an ideal picnic-spot setting by the riverside at *Skenfrith*. An even more complete castle is to be found at *Grosmont*, to the north-west.

Symonds Yat
Ye Olde Ferrie Inne

20

In any list of the beauty spots of England and Wales the lower Wye valley would surely be near the top of the list. The river enters a deep, wooded gorge, which sustains its loveliness all the way to its mouth at Chepstow.

Symonds Yat stands at the entrance to this scenic area and Ye Olde Ferrie Inne commands a strategic position on the west bank. This large hostelry is 500 years old and was once an overnight halt for bargees, in the days when this was a major traffic artery. The sun terraces, poised over the river, are extremely difficult to leave on a sunny day. Inside you will find a large lounge bar and a separate dining room, cool on hot days and cosy on cooler ones.

Turning the gaze from the river to the bar gives an almost equally appealing view. Real ales such as Morland Old Speckled Hen, Wadworth 6X, Bass, John Smith's and Theakston Best are joined by Worthington, Guinness, Caffrey's and Grolsch. Cider drinkers are not forgotten, with Strongbow and Scrumpy Jack on offer. Having decided on a drink, now look at the logically presented blackboard to assess your eating options. Starters include deep-fried crispy vegetables and scampi dip. Main courses range from jacket potatoes through Yorkshire puddings or home-cooked beef and orange pie to rump steaks. Vegetarians need not despair, with tasty spinach and ricotta cannelloni and mushroom and nut fettucini amongst their treats. Children's favourites (chicken nuggets, burgers and so on) and tempting desserts such as ginger and pineapple pudding are all on offer, so no one should be disappointed.

Summertime opening is from 11 am to 11 pm, with food available from noon to 2.15 pm and again from 6.30 pm to 9.15 pm. Don't despair if you arrive after the lunch closure, as cream teas are served during the summer months. In winter hours are more restricted – please phone ahead to check.

Telephone: 01600 890232.

How to get there: Turn off the A40 at the Whitchurch services 5½ miles south of Ross-on-Wye, signed 'Symonds Yat West'. Follow this narrowing road for almost a mile and fork left, steeply downhill, at the sign for Ye Olde Ferrie Inne.

Parking: A reasonable car park is located adjacent to the inn. There may be a charge at peak times.

Length of the walk: 3¾ miles. Map: OS Landranger 162 Gloucester and Forest of Dean area or Outdoor Leisure (1:25 000) Wye Valley and Forest of Dean (inn GR 557165).

The key to this walk is the initial crossing of the Wye by the hand ferry. The ferryman can be summoned from the inn, so you need to be there during opening hours – out of season or in bad weather please phone in advance. There follows a gentle riverside walk through this glorious valley, crossing the river by a suspension bridge to return along the opposite bank. With not too much route-finding involved you can concentrate on the scenery!

The Walk

First enter the inn and ask the ferryman to take you across the river. There will be a small fee but it will be well worth it for the experience of a hand-hauled ferry.

Once safely disembarked, turn right and follow the river bank,

93

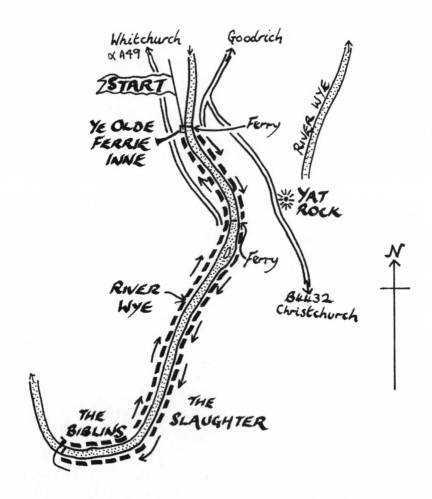

now in Gloucestershire. Pass through a caravan park and join the minor road. This will take you past the Saracen's Head Inn, the site of another ferry. Ignore the signs for the Wye Valley Walk, branching off to the left, and keep by the riverside.

On the right are the rapids of New Weir, overhung by the gates used by whitewater canoeists. Once the scene here was very different. As the 19th century began this was a thriving industrial area and at one time the New Weir Forge was the largest in Britain. The river's energy, harnessed by the weir, was the motive force behind the forge, which used iron ore from the Forest of Dean and the limestone immediately to hand. You may still find clinker from those days by the riverside.

You will now join the trackbed of the Ross to Monmouth Railway. Opened in 1873, it was never very profitable and closed in 1959. Now it makes a well-drained walking and cycling surface. The signal box was precariously poised over the river by means of two iron girders.

A little further along is an area known as The Slaughter. Not surprisingly, there are many gory stories to explain this name. Most are based upon battles, sometimes involving Vikings, sometimes Romans – or even King Arthur himself. However, the Saxon word 'sloghtre' means a muddy place, so this may be the explanation for stick in the muds.

Shortly after the junction with the Braceland and Christchurch Camp path, the Biblins suspension bridge comes into view. It was constructed by the Forestry Commission in 1957 and provides a valuable and slightly exciting river crossing. Once over, turn right, passing through the camp sites. Look out on the left for Dropping Wells, caves – formerly iron ore mines – which contain stalactites.

The river Wye.

Continuing along the path, you may catch glimpses of fallow deer patrolling the woods amongst the limestone outcrops. You will eventually pass the Woodlea Hotel and reach a road, at the apex of a hairpin bend. Go right and follow this road, perhaps more of a track, with sightings of the river. People in boats, whether canoes, rowing boats or pleasure craft, are much in evidence.

Once upon a time the river was navigable, although plagued by infamous rapids. Probably its heyday was between about 1770 and 1860, when the commercial traffic was joined by steamboats bearing tourists from Ross to Chepstow. They would disembark below Yat Rock for a picnic lunch, ascend the rock, then walk down to the opposite arm of the river's loop, where their boat would have completed the 5 mile journey to meet them.

On arriving back at Ye Olde Ferrie Inne, the most dangerous part of the walk (albeit avoidable) is the short-cut down the steep stone steps which cut through the building to lead directly to the front door.

Places of interest nearby

You want more? Well, there is more! How about the *Wye Valley Heritage Centre*, high on Doward Hill above Yat West? Here there are rural bygones, including over 100 tractors. Then there is the *Visitor Centre* at Yat West itself. Attractions include the Jubilee Maze, the World of Butterflies and tearooms. At *Yat East* is the rock, which in spring and early summer hosts the telescopes and binoculars of the RSPB so that visitors can view the peregrine falcons' nest. Nearby, to the north, is the *Wye Valley Farm Park* and *Goodrich Castle*.